BUILDING
—THE—
BODY OF CHRIST

BUILDING
—THE—
BODY OF CHRIST

LaDell Farrar

iUniverse LLC
Bloomington

Building the Body of Christ

iUniverse books may be ordered through booksellers or by contacting:

iUniverse LLC
1663 Liberty Drive
Bloomington, IN 47403
www.iuniverse.com
1-800-Authors (1-800-288-4677)

ISBN: 978-1-4917-0125-6 (sc)
ISBN: 978-1-4917-0124-9 (hc)
ISBN: 978-1-4917-0123-2 (ebk)

Library of Congress Control Number: 2013914343

Printed in the United States of America

iUniverse rev. date: 08/26/2013

Hear the word of the Lord, O children of Israel,
for the Lord has a controversy with the inhabitants of the land.
There is no faithfulness or steadfast love,
and no knowledge of God in the land . . .
My people are destroyed for lack of knowledge.

Hosea 4:1, 4:6

CONTENTS

ACKNOWLEDGMENTS

I want to give a special thank-you to all the members at the Lighthouse SDA Church in St. Louis, Missouri. In some way, they all have helped me in my spiritual journey which, by God's grace, assisted in the production of my writing.

Thank you to Pastor Joseph T. Ikner III for his examples of making prayer practical for everyone to grasp.

Also, I benefited a great deal because of the guidance, training, and support of my uncle Kenneth Williams, Lenore Harris, Jacci Davis, Professor Anne Willey, and my best friend, Shaleya Anderson. The experiences they shared led to the Holy Spirit grabbing hold of me, leading me to God's saving grace. That is when I realized that no matter how far we get ourselves lost in our web of confusion, Jesus paves a path so that we may find our way back to God. God is ever waiting for our hearts to turn to him that we may live abundantly under his umbrella of grace. Wherever we are, God sees us. Whatever we experience, God is with us. However we need him, he hears us.

And for that I say thank you, Lord and Savior, my all in all.

PROLOGUE

Back in the year 1999, my life was simple, unexciting, and frivolous. *Purpose* really had no meaning to me because things weren't what they appeared. Purpose indicated that my adult life would depend on every decision I made from that moment. I began high school that year, and as far as every freshman was concerned, adulthood was ages away.

This is a hindsight observation because—my mistake—I didn't take much of anything seriously. School, friendships, even church: none of them had a real purpose, it seemed to me, because they didn't have the direct consequences that adults foretold.

For example, I didn't value relationships as I should have. I had no true connection with anyone. The goal of education should always be to improve and rise higher. My focus, because of my lack of purpose, was just to keep up so that I wasn't left behind. As for church, my understanding was blunt. Go to church, get to heaven; don't attend church, and you've reserved a one-way ticket to hell.

Fear and respect, so I thought. The picture wasn't only brighter but also an offshoot of what I understood. For a portion of my teen life, I only tolerated attending church services. I mainly didn't care to know much about religion. My attitude clearly showcased my belief that the rules about the proper way of Christian living didn't apply to me.

Sadly, that frame of mind continued for the next ten years. Then, as God would have it, a monumental catastrophe occurred that exposed the lack of knowledge that had led me to error in just about every area.

This event occurred in 2009; it was the breakup of a companionship that had begun nearly three years earlier. Breakups, in a way, are like women. One only understands them in hindsight. So, as time advanced, I received clearer insight into and a broader perspective on why it was necessary for that relationship to collapse.

One thing I realized is that God never intends for two individuals to separate. But once the two cross forbidden boundaries and misrepresent the true image that should be in them, the only way is to get away. Forever? Only God knows.

I won't give time the credit for getting me beyond the devastation, however. What occupied my schedule during the next few years is undoubtedly worthy of all the praise. The magnitude of what I learned in just one year after my own personal D-day was greater than what I had learned over the previous ten years.

Complex discussions, behaviors, feelings, and thoughts all had rays of light reflecting on them, so much so that darkness impersonated light. Jesus mentioned something like this in Matthew 6:22–23, which meant for me that I wasn't the sharpest tool in the shed.

Nevertheless, during that year and time apart, I realized that God had used that tragedy to liberate me from the blindness that my mind was engrossed in. Here I was, a veteran church attendee in the eyes of some, taking baby steps toward learning that there is more purpose in God's plan than the decisions I made seamlessly every day.

Since that faithful D-day, each point of my life has been centered on one purpose. Collectively, it all makes perfect sense.

What I experienced through my age of darkness was no different from what I witnessed in the church soon after my deliverance. God's image was sluggishly being restored in those whom he called out of their own precepts of darkness. I saw bits and pieces of it everywhere. Broken people failing to live lives that testified to the preaching they accepted. Relationships torn by past hurt and lack of communication. Faithless hearts void of religious prayer, continually struggling to separate spiritual guidance and carnal desire. All of these situations came about by way of a lack of knowledge. The lesson that one teaches is the lesson that one needs to hear first.

The Holy Bible teaches the gospel, and the gospel speaks for itself. This is exactly how souls are won over, because the Word spreads like a virus, affecting all it touches personally to their personal benefit. These souls are then called out and into *ecclesia*, the church. They are equipped with unique gifts to minister, especially to those outside of belief, in the best way to edify the church.

The process therefore starts with the first believers, the primary representatives who faithfully take their stands for Christ. These persons are best suited for ministry because of their decisions to follow wherever God's Spirit leads them. Their service is freely given, and their lifestyles testify to God's mercy, grace, and victory through his Son, Jesus.

Those souls were once hostile to the Light, friends of the world and darkness. Those souls were workers of iniquity, but only for a season, until the Word of Life buried their disgraced passions. Those are the same souls that were once like my own. They are the main reason why I chose to explore six delicate topics to rebuild the very character that God ordained for everyone to acquire.

Like myself, these topics will be tested and tried like gold through the fire. They will not be made perfect overnight, but will persevere and endure for a moment that is rarely caught by the eye, once the last person has the opportunity to decide to accept or reject this calling.

I am called to reach the souls that are hostile to the Light so that they may resume their positions in Christ's body of believers, building and edifying one another to hasten the return of our Redeemer. In order to build this body of believers, each individual must reach that arrival point, that starting spot in the marathon for perfection.

My gambit is this book: six unforgettable areas that shape a personality. Once a soul has been informed about these topics and has applied these insights, the soul's estimated time of arrival will be reduced and personal ministry will be broadened. Undoubtedly this will be to the advantage of the entire body of believers, after each character is built by Christ first.

CHAPTER 1

Epistle on Relationships

When a relationship starts, the focus is usually on prolonging the interaction—to have an overall successful union. People may believe that their foundational support comes from their inner beings, and that they can control the outcome. However, what supports a relationship should also be what supports the individual. Christ, as always, should be at the center of everything, even before a new relationship begins.

It can be easily said that relationships are about connecting, associating, and being involved, typically with another living thing. One can understand how different everyday interactions can seem from one another, because of the number of connections we typically have. In order to make any relationship improve and then be successful, all parties involved must possess several characteristics, primarily patience, effective communication, trust, honesty, and compassion.

The downfall for a connection is failure to uphold any one of these characteristics, which could trigger a breaking point in one's involvement. No matter if it is by mistake or intentionally, a breaking point damages an individual's trust, which in turn leaves an open wound in a person's heart—a wound that will continue to be exposed until healed properly.

The sad thing is that it's common to trigger breaking points in relationships because people are not always equipped with the tools for an effective relationship. In some fashion, we all have learned society's proposal of how to be successfully separate from all others; this is the "law of self." We're taught to depend on, rely on, trust in, and seek within ourselves for everything we dream and work for. The law of self can be seen all over television, in our workplaces, and even in our homes.

Society's design can grasp us like a parasite and influence egotistical behavior so that we will even avoid a social life to pursue our dreams. Self-centered behavior places an expiration date on relationships, never allowing them to mature.

The ideal should be that, once I establish a connection with another person I want to grow and mature with, I no longer think solely of myself, my benefits, or my own way of thinking. Acceptance of another as much as I accept myself is what I should believe and strive for. Society hides this truth. The law of self destroys community, trampling friendships by misidentifying people as stepping stones or motivational devices.

Thankfully, there is a way to break the law of self by adopting another, which is God's law.

STARTING WITH GOD

In fact, one must begin with God in order to know how to be in and continue through a sustaining relationship. Yes, God—but why God? What I have found to be true is that it takes God to institute a relationship because he instigated the art of involvement long before human contact. Without God, the foundation of every relationship I held crumbled at some point; many left me with nothing to hold myself together. A large portion of my time was driven by the consequences for my actions and the amount of reconciliation needed to repair relationship breaks.

I now focus on preventive measures rather than expecting and accepting failures. With God's guidance, my connections are better than I could ever have imagined. Every relationship-enhancing quality that I lacked was gift wrapped and displayed within me once my relationship with God became fruitful. After I realized what was happening to me as a result in accepting God's law into my life, I appreciated how vital God is in human contact.

I'm enlightened even more about God's position while I review Adam's story in the garden of Eden. Every bit of what was necessary to Adam's life was in the garden before he was created. Then grace was given later once God gave him a partner. Adam never requested companionship; either he was ignorant of what a connection could bring to his life or he was so intrigued by everything that his Father placed before him that it never came up.

Whatever the case, God saw that relationship would be better for Adam personally. On the next day, the seventh day, God set a time for rest and reflection. This time was set apart from every other day and duty so that the work of God's hands would benefit in relationship with him without any distractions. In that, God began to show himself not only as God the Creator, but also as Abba-Father, Jehovah-Jireh (the provider), and Emmanuel (God with us). So as Adam was created on the sixth day and found God as a loving and pure maker on the seventh day, Adam's compliance with his duties in the garden was obedience by way of love for God, with whom Adam found a relationship.

The symbol of God's relationship is his day of rest, which gives all of his creation the entire span of that day to get to further know its Creator. This shows us that God is able to see past every outcome and situation and provide what is best for our lives. It is extremely beneficial knowing God as our provider, being primarily fulfilled in him. This knowledge teaches us that we should not be contented in the things or people we are blessed with. We should be the givers. God shows us that the bonds we hold are purest when we establish relationship first with him. Unions that are void of this spiritual foundation often cause grief, discomfort, and even regret, which make it difficult for anyone striving to form lasting attachments.

Adam took his mind, heart, and eyes off of God once, and that lapse caused a detrimental outcome. Learning from Adam's mistake, we see that apart from God, there is a selfishness that inhabits us all. We've all inherited that fallen nature. This nature drives our thoughts and wills toward doing what feels right at the time rather than what is truly correct behavior.

That nature will only be repaired through acceptance of Christ's works. The prophet Isaiah wrote to God's people, "Behold, the Lord's hand is not shortened, that it cannot save, or his ear dull, that it cannot hear; but your iniquities have made a separation between you and your God, and your sins have hidden his face from you so that he does not hear" (Isaiah 59:1–2). Because of that nature, we make flawed decisions that bring agonizing results to our lives, which will put a strain on our relationships.

A tainted mind is driven by a heart with self-centered intentions. God, through the prophet Ezekiel, stretches his hand forward with this promise: "I will sprinkle clean water on you, and you shall be clean from all your uncleanness, and from all your idols I will cleanse you. And I will give you a new heart, and a new spirit I will put within you. And I will remove the heart of stone from your flesh and give you a heart of flesh. And I will put my Spirit within you, and cause you to walk in my statutes and be careful to obey my rules" (Ezekiel 36:25–27).

Though we may fall short, the plea God makes to us to turn away from disobedience is heartfelt. What God is offering is sufficient to keep us from falling. It will enable us to fully surrender our lives to him. We are guaranteed the ability to please God and wholeheartedly benefit others in everything we choose, being influenced by his Spirit.

REACHING OUT TO GOD

When it comes to extending one's will, the saying "Draw near to God, and he will draw near to you" is the direct approach. However, this methodology, while practical, seems paradoxical due to the stipulations that are needed to convert. In order for one to accept God's ways, the mind has to elect against itself—to give up its drive and serve, rather than create possibilities from self-perception. One must unlearn every secular, self-taught perspective and adopt truth, even when one's thoughts and actions are well suited to everyday situations.

Human nature accepts a way of making it through life that's suited to one's lifestyle. No two people think and act identically. God is basically stating that, though you "feel" you have brought yourself thus far, you should understand there is a way better than your own. Through this other way, you'll be taken to a higher plane mentally, spiritually, and psychologically (and sometimes even physically).

This is not what the average adult wants to hear. The question is why, though—why wouldn't someone want to change things up a bit? The answer is that change, with God, consists of a complete transformation rather than a small touch-up. Maybe it's a trust issue, fear, or stubbornness, but whatever the case, we struggle to implement someone else's plan for our lives without leaving anything of self for self.

Personality is what makes up a person. The human psyche is made to protect identity based on the self's morals, values, and way of life. Taking a look at our own lives, a question that must be asked is, did the way that we adapted work out for us in coping with whatever the day brought us? Was there ever a time when we had to adjust rather than being consistent in applying our personal theories? Is there something that we still don't quite have the answer to?

Without God, it's simple to drift from one way of thinking to the next. A lot of things may make sense for a given moment. Who will tell us we are wrong? Truth is often viewed as proof that something works.

God knows that he is the way, the truth, and the life. The problem is that an unbeliever doesn't have concrete evidence to know that. An unbeliever has to step outside of every practical chain of reasoning, trusting first before really knowing what is to come later.

In my own life, my pride was the catalyst that forbade a true relationship with God. I lacked character. In every involvement I had with friends and family, I failed to realize that what works for one person isn't going to work for a random second person. My sister, for instance, loves our relationship because we're honest with each other. The give/take ratio is enough to keep both of us satisfied, but that came through time and adjustment to one another.

What God is offering is universal sufficiency. When one is dependent on him, trusting and obeying, one is not left to perform obscure tasks toward unattainable goals. Anything is possible when one is on God's side. One may not have quite what one wants, but will have exactly what is vital for life.

Someone once told me that I was selfish. She described it as a lack of equity in our relationship. I lacked the character to care about and reciprocate feelings and attention. Yes, I wanted to and believed that I could, otherwise I probably wouldn't have been in a relationship. But I was hurting her and damaging the trust she had placed in me. She had no opportunity to heal from past hurts due to the constant burden of mistrust.

Confronting the reality of her pain struck me even harder than those words. But no matter how willing I was or the amount of effort I put in, I continued to administer unintended hurt. I could not try without failing. Finally, I realized that I should give up trying.

Back then, I had no idea of how to keep from hurting someone. But then how could I? Promising that I would never do anything hurtful again was similar to promising to personally fix an engine I had blown out. I'm no mechanic; I purchase gas and oil changes. Before Christ (BC) I had no way to completely care for anyone as much as I did myself, because I came first in every situation in my life.

When I accepted Jesus in my heart, I gave up everything that had previously commanded my deepest feelings—things like egoism, cynicism, fear, and insecurity. My goal was complete commitment to Christ without giving up or turning back. BC, my selfish reputation preceded me, but during my Christian journey I realized where my attention was truly focused. I began to see where change was needed. As a result of my revelation, I was affirmed encouragingly rather than shamed.

Without the most important relationship in my life developing day by day, anyone would have been at the mercy of my narcissism. Looking back at what God could have done for me in those days—where I could have been, what I could have been in character, and the things that I could have accomplished by his grace—I am made speechless. I can only offer praise because of the many second chances he provides.

We have to reach out to God constantly on our Christian journey to perfection. Every error, wrong, and misconception will come to light as we adopt the righteousness that God offers. God's law is proven perfect because it gives clear sight of the personality to come. It's not a one-time or once-in-a-while effort. After the Holy Spirit exposes faults and shortcomings and shows the way of blameless behavior, our instinctive old selves will attempt to resurface.

Therefore, just as we call our loved ones and engage in their lives, we must also allow our Father to engage in our lives. We only know others by strengthening the connection between us and them. The same concept applies with God. Improving our personal relationships with him will come by understanding the gospel.

A sermon has a reliable place in our spiritual lives, but does not equal the understanding gained through personal Bible study. Another's personal testimony provides great encouragement but alone will not allow God to show up in our lives the way individual devotion will. Our Lord wants to be the first one to hear from us because he cares about absolutely everything. "But even the hairs of your head are all numbered" (Matthew 10:30). Prayer enforces communication with God.

There is a correct way to pray as well as an accurate way to grasp the purpose of prayer. Think of prayer as opening the door to your issues, concerns, and thoughts. God is able to add to and remove from your storehouse of issues through that open door. Another way to see prayer is as your flare gun to use when life leaves you stranded. Shoot the flare toward the sky, and God's light will illuminate the situation.

Jesus explained exactly what should happen during a praying session. According to Luke, there should be *praise and worship* to acknowledge God for who he is. "And he said to them, 'when you pray, say: Father, hallowed be your name'" (Luke 11:2). There should be *relinquishment* by requesting God's will be done above anything else: "Your Kingdom come" (Luke 11:2). (Matthew 6:10 adds "your will be done.") There should be *pleading* for our own needs and blessings for others: "Give us each day our daily bread" (Luke 11:3). There should be *confession* along with the request for a forgiving heart: "and forgive us our sins, for we ourselves forgive everyone who is indebted to us" (Luke 11:4). There should be an acknowledgment of the need for God's *deliverance and protection*: "and lead us not into temptation" (Luke 11:4). (Matthew 6:13 adds, "But deliver us from evil.")

In addition to this, we should be praying for the *promises* that God offers (e.g., Psalm 37:4, "Delight yourself in the Lord, and he will give you the desires of your heart.") We must likewise uphold the *faith* that it will happen just as he said it will: "But let him ask in faith, with no doubting, for the one who doubts is like a wave of the seas that is driven and tossed by the wind" (James 1:6). An additional text that we can rely on in our prayers is 1 John 5:14: "And this is the confidence that we have toward him, that if we ask anything according to his will he hears us."

Before I understood and accepted this formula for prayer, I constantly struggled with communicating with God, requesting what I thought was important. I saw God moving around me, but my eyes weren't directly on him to notice what was happening specifically for me. Confused, I could only guess that I had God on my side. I didn't realize that because of God's authority, I should have been on God's side. Despite that lack of confidence, I continued praying. This experience was similar to the time when I thought I understood what a relationship was.

BC, I would go from one relationship to the next, asserting that I felt the pure touch of God inside of me, which is love. However I continued showing only partial signs of loving acts. I tried supplementing this "love" with the alternative "tough love," but love is complete all by itself. There is not a regular love we can claim and then a "true" love that is greater. Before my saving grace I would utter the words "I love you," giving them freely with no ability to uphold one standard that governs love's name.

Later, after studying the Bible, I was flabbergasted. I did not have a clue about love. Not only that, but I was unaware of any emotion that I held for anyone. I couldn't decipher love from obsession, kindness from a simple scheme, or envy from hatred. But when the Light removed darkness, I was no longer unaware of what love is. I stood steps closer to improving my relationships.

In the same way, I had a much better time and experience in prayer once I understood its purpose.

REAL LOVE

The words *love* and *God* are interchangeable (1 John 4:8: "Anyone who does not love does not know God, because God is love"). Therefore, neither word should be taken carelessly in the slightest sense. For God so loved the world that he gave, and he keeps on giving. He nourishes us with fresh supplies of himself daily, that we may then spread him (love) to everyone that we encounter. That supply of everlasting pureness is vital to our relationships. Without it, our involvement with others can end or be completely in vain. When love is buried deep inside of our hearts, then watered and cared for, we can break off portions of that love and give freely without expecting much in return.

I realized the truth in that statement because BC, whenever I used the word *love*, I expected to get whatever I wanted, not always what the other person was willing to give. What I learned in that mistake is that love is not a feeling that we have and then lose. Yes, it brings forth feelings and emotions, but is not one of those. More times than not, when I used the word *love*, what I really meant was *infatuation, passion*, or *admiration*.

God's Word, in the commonly known passage 1 Corinthians 13, simply says that "Love is patient" (v. 4). *Patience* is allowing someone to act imperfectly. Often we have high standards and expectations. We don't endure those who don't meet our requirements. But love, in fact, is patient.

Corinthians also says that love is kind. *Kindness* can be defined as compassion: simply noticing someone, recognizing their need, and even going out of your way to help meet that need.

"Love does not envy or boast" (v. 4) means that one must not feel discontent or covetousness regarding others' advantages, possessions, or attainments. Envy is one of the most potent causes of unhappiness. Love has no room for speaking excessively about oneself. Rather, it opposes self-praise.

"It is not arrogant or rude" (v. 4–5). This means love is not boldly disrespectful in speech or behavior and also is not discourteous. "It does not insist on its own way" (v. 5). *Egoism* is the tendency to be self-centered, considering only one's own interest out of conceit.

"It is not irritable or resentful" (v. 5). This includes being easily annoyed, provoked, or short-tempered. Showing displeasure toward someone from a sense of being injured or offended is *resentment*.

"It does not rejoice at wrong doing, but rejoices with truth" (v. 6). Love won't give praise to that which can cause hurt or pain, but will support and lift upward. "Love bears all things" (v. 7) means that love sustains burdens, takes care of others, and is tolerant.

"Believes all things, hopes all things, endures all things. Love never ends" (v. 7–8). There is absolutely no circumstance when love is no longer there, because when there is love (God) inside of us, then we will ever have love for others.

My lack of understanding of love prevented me from maturing in any relationship. I was moving backward from any breaking point I faced, breaking points such as mistrust, emotions colliding, the inability to agree, or whatever else challenged my low self-esteem. All of those breaking points caused me to withdraw into myself, which damaged my ability to connect.

Now that I recognize my ability to love and know exactly how to fulfill commitment because of Christ, my relationships have stability. I expect less and give much more than I ever thought to before. All praises be to God for what he does in order to allow me to come together in the most fervent fellowship with just about anyone in my life. The majority and the most memorable testimonies and blessings that I've experienced were those that involved me thinking less of myself and more for someone else. "Do nothing from selfish ambition or conceit, but in humility count others more significant than yourselves" (Philippians 2:3).

I notice that as my dependency on Christ's lessons grows, selfishness decreases and revelations increase. Accepting Jesus's way of being in relationship with others means loving even the unlovable.

> You have heard that it was said, "You shall love your neighbor and hate your enemy." But I say to you, Love your enemies and pray for those who persecute you, so that you may be sons of your Father who is in heaven. For he makes his sun rise on the evil and on the good and sends rain on the just and on the unjust. For if you love those who love you, what reward do

> you have? Do not even the tax collectors do the same?
> And if you greet only your brothers, what more are you
> doing than others? Do not even the Gentiles do the
> same? You therefore must be perfect, as your heavenly
> Father is perfect. (Matthew 5:43–48)

It is completely impossible to have one of these genuine relationships without the other key component—forgiveness. I agree, there is almost no better feeling than having someone you love so much love you in return. Most times, we are content with just having someone who agrees with us. But when a friend appears to be a threatening enemy or, even worse, a family member, how does one deal with this scenario?

The Word tells us, "For if you forgive others their trespasses, your heavenly Father will also forgive you" (Matthew 6:14). This direction sounds difficult to perform, and frankly we can't without Christ's help. It takes Christ to forgive. In my own experience, I was not able on my own to grant pardon for an offense, let alone cease to feel resentment. This means that I didn't give any measure of forgiveness until I realized the amount that I've been forgiven through my faith in the grace that God gives me.

One strategy for forgiving, or even not having to ask someone to be forgiven later, is found in Matthew:

> Judge not, that you be not judged. For with the
> judgment you pronounce you will be judged, and with
> the measure you use it will be measured to you. Why
> do you see the speck that is in your brother's eye, but
> do not notice the log that is in your own eye? Or how
> can you say to your brother, "Let me take the speck out
> of your eye," when there is the log in your own eye?
> You hypocrite, first take the log out of your own eye,
> and then you will see clearly to take the speck out of
> your brother's eye. (Matthew 7:1–5)

Forgiveness provides hope, and hope is what motivates a person to strive toward success. In this case, success is reconciliation. Love is not complete without forgiveness. Relationships are whole when there is love binding them.

ULTIMATE RELIEF

At this stage of enlightenment, we should no longer express ourselves in the old manner because there is a bigger, broader picture. Our fallen natures prove that people are full of imperfections and are helpless. On our own, we do not behave as God requires even on our best days.

After receiving God's fulfillment, we are commanded to share what we have gained and lead others into the same loving relationship with Christ, that they may be made whole as well. The unions we form thereafter will become 100 percent pure, abiding by his statutes and relying completely upon Christ living inside us. As God's perfect law sets the boundaries in each person's life, those standards will allow the connections between couples, families, and friends to become exceptional.

CHAPTER 2

Communication: Threefold

After we have accepted that the feeling is mutual, like in any relationship, we move toward frequent communication. Not everyone is outgoing and open to talking. Despite that, we can all learn from God's Word what communication should ultimately look like, making listening and speaking a true success.

It's hilarious now when I think about how important communication was to me in my former days. Connecting and communicating, I came to realize, is a continuous cycle and because both were relevant, I failed to see that this was the key to connections. How silly was I? After studying God's Word, I realized how to communicate effectively. Communication is more than performing the word. It's not merely talking, but rather how you talk. More than listening, it's how well you listen.

Expression keeps everything in perspective. Yes, I may have conveyed the message that I needed to, but if I didn't express myself properly, my statement may not have been presented in the fashion that I intended. In all fairness, I was correct in believing that communication is the most vital attribute for developing a relationship. The issue is that effectively communicating is not everyone's aim. I have noticed that we as a society can be relatively passive, whether by not giving thorough explanations or by showing little, if any, reaction to people or experiences.

This is evidence that we are making assumptions, a habit that negates communication's genuineness. I've often felt like resigning from interaction with certain people because of their assumptions. Text-talk, relaying information by way of someone else, vague responses, or even no response can all lead to the target of communication making assumptions about your meaning. If the situation matters enough, the person you are supposed to be communicating with might be forced to finding the answer on his or her own. When two or more are involved in anything, they shouldn't be figuring things out alone.

No matter what the situation, communication is one of the most valuable aspects of relational involvement. Communicating effectively is a healthy way to avoid stress.

ARTICULATE

The idea of communication is strictly to convey a message. At times, we may have to ponder what needs to be said, the information that's relevant to making our conversation productive. It's a great idea to know how to speak. "Let your speech always be gracious, seasoned with salt, so that you may know how you ought to answer each person" (Colossians 4:6). It's not a coincidence that Paul uses the term *salt*. Jesus used that term as well, explaining that his followers are "the salt of the earth" (Matthew 5:13). Just about every living thing needs salt in some way.

Salt is an antibacterial—it prevents bacteria from growing, which is why salt is used as a preservative. In Paul's context we see the correlation that we are to preserve, or purposely prevent decay in, the unity we have as humans. Our compassion, kindness, truth, knowledge, and other traits should be illustrated by our choice of words. If we hold fast to this principle, then we'll indeed preserve and not tear down, enrich and not deplete our relationships.

This gives witness to the text Peter wrote: "Finally, all of you, have unity of mind, sympathy, brotherly love, a tender heart, and a humble mind. Do not repay evil for evil or reviling for reviling, but on the contrary, bless, for to this you were called that you may obtain a blessing" (1 Peter 3:8–9). The wisdom that we are given, by grace, should be upheld so that we will respond to everyone correctly, thus exhibiting God's complete goodness.

Jesus made such a correct response to those who tried to twist the lessons of the law. A lawyer approached Jesus and asked, "Which is the great commandment in the Law?" (Matthew 22:36). The purpose of the question was to test Jesus's knowledge and to see if he would belittle the entirety of the law the Israelites had received from God. If Jesus were to identify one commandment as greater than any other, it would mean that Jesus was claiming one commandment was enough; grace would still be given without adhering to the entire law, and therefore the rest of the law was not perfect.

Jesus's answer was, "You shall love the Lord your God with all your heart and with all your soul and with all your mind. This is the great and first commandment. And a second is like it: You shall love your neighbor as yourself. On these two commandments depend all the Law and the Prophets" (Matthew 22:37–40).

His response combined commandments one through four as first (meaning that there is at least one more) and great, dealing with the relationship that God and his creation are meant to have. The second compiled the last six commandments, which deal with human relationships. His reply was well thought and accurate.

The first part of thinking before we speak is to understand that absolutely no one can read minds. There can be plenty of confusion as the result of processing thoughts, then converting them into speech. When two or more individuals come together in discussion, all are projecting, perceiving, and thinking at different paces. No two people will consistently have the same thoughts, understanding, or solution. It's imperative that each of us take time to express ourselves to others until they understand, and to listen until we understand others.

Context is the key in speaking. Without a proper understanding of the context, a lesson can have any type of meaning, and who would be wrong when explaining what a statement "truly" means?

A person I'll name Dexter and another I'll name Jillian found an issue in their relationship. Dexter and Jillian interacted with one another on several occasions, but Dexter had no idea how Jillian truly felt about him. Jillian was repulsed by some things about Dexter, but due to a lack of communication, Dexter never found out. So of course the problem continued and Dexter's image declined in the eyes of Jillian.

Though she didn't speak directly to Dexter about it, Jillian went outside their circle of involvement and mentioned the problem to a third party, Curtis. Curtis received all the emotions, lectures, and information that Dexter should have been receiving. It was Curtis, not Jillian, who eventually made it clear to Dexter how Jillian felt about him.

Instead of accepting the information from Curtis the way it was intended, Dexter resented the communication because nothing had ever been presented to him by Jillian. This led to the collapse of not only Dexter and Jillian's relationship, but Dexter and Curtis's as well.

As Christians, we have God's voice ever speaking to us. Without context and understanding, we'll miss the mark every time we are put to the test.

Matthew's gospel also has a lesson on this theme. "If your brother sins against you, go and tell him his fault, between you and him alone. If he listens to you, you have gained your brother. But if he does not listen, take one or two others along with you, that every charge may be established by the evidence of two or three witnesses" (Matthew 18:15-16). This passage speaks clearly to us about dealing with situations like the one among Jillian, Dexter, and Curtis. When God talks, we must always take his words and apply them directly to the context in which he is speaking. In my opinion, there aren't any good reasons for withholding applicable information. We must be thorough rather than partial so that we don't misuse our time.

One last thought about speech is the declaration of our will or duties in reference to the future. Promises, whether made in response to another's request or simply announced, should always be upheld to the best of our ability. To speak and then mistakenly or carelessly not maintain a promise causes others to consider us liars. "But above all, my brothers, do not swear, either by heaven or by earth or by any other oath, but let your 'yes' be yes and your 'no' be no, so that you may not fall under condemnation" (James 5:12).

EXPRESSION

Imagine that when you speak, there is someone cautiously listening, and you say the correct statement the wrong way. To that person it might seem as though you were intentionally being offensive.

To accommodate our listeners, we should express our feelings by using proper tone of voice and body language, demonstrating gracious speech. David, in Psalm 19:14, wrote this prayer/lesson that speaks volumes on the boundaries of acceptable expression: "Let the words of my mouth and the meditation of my heart be acceptable in your sight, O Lord, my rock and my redeemer."

Jesus explained it's what's inside of a person that causes what comes out to be inappropriate. The issue he was asked about was washing hands before eating, but the message was deeper. "Hear and understand: it is not what goes into the mouth that defiles a person, but what comes out of the mouth: this defiles a person" (Matthew 15:10–11). Knowing the truth in Jesus's statement will enlighten us on the purpose of David's psalm. Praying before we speak, especially David's prayer, can remind us of where we should be.

Handing over our emotions to God is to our advantage because he is undisputed at removing negative traits from our lives. Clearly prayer is powerful, and knowing what to pray for is better. Throw in works that give witness to one's faith, and there is an even better strategy for proper expression.

Frankly, we all are in need of understanding, compassion, humility, patience, and gentleness (Galatians 5:22–23). These are a few of the qualities the Holy Spirit offers to help us deal with the adversarial potential of person-to-person relations. Some people carry baggage everywhere. Others have plenty of disgraceful experiences and make those horrible facts known at the drop of a hat. Such displays of flawed character can exhaust us. We may respond by frowning, casting a sharp eye, and even slandering the ones we scorn. A negative message is sent.

A text that will enlighten our way of thinking before and during stressful interactions is Galatians 3:28: "There is neither Jew nor Greek, there is neither slave nor free, there is no male and female, for you are all one in Christ Jesus." Because all are one in Christ, we shouldn't think of ourselves as any greater than anyone else. Whether we realize it or not, God has a plan for absolutely everyone, not just those following him. "So speak and so act as those who are to be judged under the law of liberty" (James 2:12).

The objective is "so that you may know how you ought to answer each person" (Colossians 4:6). Strictly think before acting.

Grief, endearment, excitement, and astonishment are only a few emotions that we express. These are acceptable while speaking because they give life to our words. This is why face-to-face interaction stands above interaction like texting or passing messages, which lead to assumptions. (Parables are great ways to express feeling as well.)

However, it is necessary to limit the amount of emotion that we express. We are often unable to handle our emotions. Not governing our emotions can unleash a mass breakdown, leading to a pity party, which makes any conversation uneasy. I have realized that whatever trauma is in one's subconscious can be relieved by Jesus's healing touch. This is where peace, patience, and self-control are unquestionably important. If it is peace that we need, then peace is what Jesus promised. "Peace I leave with you; my peace I give to you. Not as the world gives do I give to you. Let not your hearts be troubled, neither let them be afraid" (John 14:27).

It is perfectly fine to express even our deepest emotions, which by now should be explicable. Rejecting what we feel is no way to handle our issues. Self-control, from the Holy Spirit, equips us with the knowledge of what to do with those emotions. Jesus, in the garden of Gethsemane, petitioned the Father in agony, expressing the most vulnerable of emotions (Mark 14:32–41). On the cross, when Jesus no longer felt the presence of God with him, "Jesus cried with a loud voice, 'Eloi, Eloi, lema sabachthani?' which means, 'My God, my God, why have you forsaken me?'" (Mark 15:34).

In distress and in confusion, we usually have the right to present the issue directly without withholding what we feel. That's where gentleness has a place, because it helps identify any issue without getting out of line.

There are statements that we can apply in such cases without going overboard with emotions. These are "I" statements that explain what "I" am feeling, what "I" am thinking, and what "I" understand. Speak for yourself. Abandon the "you" statements to avoid the perception that you are judging someone else. Not everyone handles constructive criticism well.

We need love, kindness, and goodness in order to comply with the text, "Do nothing from rivalry or conceit, but in humility count others more significant than yourselves. Let each of you look not only to his own interest, but also to the interest of others" (Philippians 2:3–4). Extend attention to others, not to yourself, so that you lead by example.

HEED

"He who has ears to hear, let him hear" (Matthew 11:15). Listening requires patience—an upgraded level of patience. We need to allow others to finish not only their words, but their thoughts as well. Typically we feel that our own thoughts are just as important, and that we know when to speak. It's very important to realize that the second we begin speaking, we are no longer listening.

Most people want someone who is going to listen. Even if advice is requested, in all reality, deep down people just want to be heard. Plan on paying attention quietly and patiently. "Know this my beloved brothers: let every person be quick to hear, slow to speak, slow to anger" (James 1:19).

When we take the time to listen, questions may be answered without ever having to be asked. Not everyone goes directly to their destination. Some like to take the scenic route, in conversation as well as in their cars, and take us on a ride. A few favor presenting their information and driving the point home, and then they are finished. Praise God for them! Others aren't so quick to finish. Some of God's children are long-winded, loquacious at heart, and emotional beings. These people must present their stories thoroughly and may even draw a word picture, describing in detail the event. Accepting that someone wants to vent can position them to relax and think clearly.

It may flat-out hurt inside when we sit and listen to someone. Humility can be removed, religion lost, and salvation put to the test. I have felt that I was boiling inside because I desired to cut another's words short and speak out of turn. That's when I realized the importance of meekness in communication. Without meekness, I didn't realize how inconsiderate I was when I began speaking intemperately. When we diminish the adrenaline and listen, we become more effective in our communicating. When we apprehend another's words, we are apt to give better advice.

Colossians 3:13 tells us to forgive: "Bearing with one another and, if one has a complaint against another, forgiving each other; as the Lord has forgiven you, so you also must forgive." Those who are meek will understand forgiveness. This was not something I wanted to hear. In conversation, often what was said offended me deeply because of the way it was expressed. I learned what Paul meant by forgiving as the Lord forgave.

Romans 5:8 testifies, "But God shows his love for us in that while we were still sinners, Christ died for us." That means that Christ accepted chastisement for what we did and continue to do. He forgave because his punishment would have been in vain had he chosen to withhold forgiveness. He forgave, which led him to request that his Father forgive as well (Luke 23:24). Christ forgave that we also may forgive and have a burden lifted from us.

Things seem and are often viewed by us as personal, but other people are not wholly focused on us. The spiritual warfare that's being waged (Ephesians 6:12) means we get caught in some crossfire. Communicate with God for his forgiveness. Once we are forgiven, we learn to cease placing blame, not holding anything against anyone. When the test arrives, our victory will build us; we will give witness to God's spirit working in us, "both to will and to work for his good pleasure" (Philippians 2:13).

CHAPTER 3

Most Valuable Prayer

When we accept God's way of life, exercising faith to the fullest while fulfilling the law in our speech toward others and our Lord, we can become the most important person this earth has ever seen—the Most Valuable Prayer that we can be. We will enter into everlasting communion as God intended.

The easiest measure of being a Christian is not initially the part where we pray. Sadly, many people are brought low, sometimes years after accepting Christ, when they reach a breaking point at which a stronger prayer life is mandatory. Realizing my own need for prayer sent me on a search to understand both prayer and why was I was neglecting it.

"None is righteous, no, not one; no one understands; no one seeks for God" (Romans 3:10–11). Paul's objective is to bring attention to God's unchanging law because some have abandoned the call of the Savior. "Now we know that whatever the law says it speaks to those who are under the law" (Romans 3:19). Paul has in mind Psalm 14:2, which reads, "The Lord looks down from heaven on the children of man, to see if there are any who understand, who seek after God."

Could this be—that there is not one who understands? When did the minds of God's people become so tainted that they do not seek him? The answer lies in the beginning of it all, when man realized that he had a mind of his own.

In Genesis chapter 3, Adam, after being encouraged by his wife, performed an advanced cognitive process: exercising the power of choice. He realized he had the freedom not to choose God's way, but to develop his own. Before eating the fruit, Adam was a being. After eating it, he noticed himself as a naked being (v. 7). At that moment of disobedience, it was as if God was no longer with him, because though his eyes were opened, he became lost within his thoughts.

Adam could have easily cried out and made his request known; instead he fell deeper into transgression's trap. Once one has sinned, one becomes an enemy of God, a solo artist, apart, and the children of men inherited that. When our eyes are off Jesus, lust to seek our own way is placed in our hearts. We become frozen in self-dependency rather than seeking divine deliverance. Adam's heart would not allow him to welcome God's presence; therefore he hid himself, and so did the men who came later.

I fell into a similar trap, believing that, because I had God on my side, I could venture out and attempt to handle things semisolo. Sometimes ignorance will open a space for humility if intellect doesn't.

"Then you will call upon me and come and pray to me, and I will hear you. You will seek me and find me, when you seek me with all your heart" (Jeremiah 29:12–13). God calls us to seek him with hearts filled with humility. The reverent relationship between God and man is that of Creator and creation, Master and servant. This is the acknowledgment that God's people should make when seeking his counsel. When we acknowledge God's unequaled and unmatched authority and call upon it, that is *prayer*.

Christian prayer recognizes exactly who is being prayed to. God spoke and the universe became what it is today. God decided to use his hands to create the first human. This God is who we pray to. When an individual tells God that there is none other to be called on or trusted in solving a matter, that individual gives our heavenly Father honor and praise. Most importantly, that acknowledgment can only be achieved when the heart creates an open space for God to occupy. God's presence is as necessary as oxygen; we are left gasping if we are without a touch from above. "As a deer pants for flowing streams, so pants my soul for you, O God" (Psalm 42:1).

"If my people who are called by my name humble themselves, and pray and seek my face and turn from their wicked ways, then I will hear from heaven and will forgive their sin and heal their land" (2 Chronicles 7:14). This passage gravitated me to the question, will God actually turn his ear from my prayers?

In actuality, I learned that God's Word speaks of repentance (Matthew 3:2, 3:8), which means to turn completely away from whatever makes us lawless. In addition to that is the text "And this is the confidence we have in him, that if we ask anything according to his will he hears us" (1 John 5:14–15). In summary, God won't do what we won't allow him to do, which makes certain prayers pointless.

Look at this concept like the gift of salvation. John 3:16 and 2 Peter 3:9 both make it clear that God's gift is for everyone who wants it. The fact that some don't receive that gift doesn't mean

God didn't intend it for them; they merely didn't do their parts to acquire it.

BC, I prayed and didn't receive the harvest of my petitions. I knew something was off, and I continued learning.

God requires sincerity in one's heart. Check.

A double-minded servant with an alternate agenda, obscuring God's plan, whether boldly or in secret, does not receive an answer to his prayer. Double check.

No one holding on to his fleshy desires, seeking personal gain or pleasure, is fully submissive to the plan, steps, and purpose that God has placed before his chosen. Ouch.

The petitions of those preoccupied with fleshy desires are self-focused. Those petitioners are, figuratively, looking to press a button and receive benefits. God's Spirit will only fill a cleared area, not one that is occupied. The Holy Spirit couldn't have said it better.

I wasn't effective in my prayer life because there was no eviction of my selfish plans from my inner being. All I was seeking were those selfish blessings that rendered my prayers irrelevant. There is absolutely no way to work for God when one is self-employed. "If I had cherished iniquity in my heart, the Lord would not have listened" (Psalm 66:18).

On the other hand, "Evening and morning and at noon I utter my complaint and moan, and he hears my voice" (Psalm 55:17). When we lift our requests to God, he is ready to hear us. There should be an earnest heart to pray during times of sorrow or need. Fervent prayer matures when we speak to God religiously, so allow your efforts to be instinctive. Paul's advice, "pray without ceasing" (1 Thessalonians 5:17), shows there is no downtime in praying, no reason not to seek God's presence and wisdom. Paul encourages us to consult with God at all times for the growth that we are in constant need of. Then God will construct us, his creation, through the promises in his Word concerning prayer. Prayer transports us nearer to God's throne of grace.

Faithful prayer, for us, should quiet any doubt concerning God's plan and attentiveness. Comfort should conquer any anxiety in our patience. Prayer allows God to place before us his divine design, revealing his authority and creating an exclusive kinship that strengthens his bond with us. Prayer returns God's children to his loving arms, because prayer is all about trusting God.

Why would we pray if we have no belief that God can and will do it? Are we so much like the father of the boy with the unclean spirit that we secretly say to our Lord, "But if you can do anything, have compassion on us and help us" (Mark 9:22). This is as much to say, "I believe that you helped others, but are you able to do something for me?" The rebuke Jesus gave this father makes it plain: "'If you can'! All things are possible for one who believes" (Mark 9:23).

"Likewise the Spirit helps us in our weakness. For we do not know what to pray for as we ought, but the Spirit himself intercedes for us with groanings too deep for words" (Romans 8:26). The Holy Spirit, when it comes, does for us what even Jesus could not do. The Spirit comes to fill a void so that God's plan is unmistakably understood. We are lost if the Spirit finds pride and selfishness, because pride and selfishness do not leave any room for the Spirit to enter and give guidance. If someone is seeking God, the Spirit has already moved on that person's behalf, but iniquity will make a separation from God (Isaiah 59:2), which will void the Holy Ghost's power.

Our hope is fulfilled when we delight in the Lord, finding ourselves in harmony with his plans, being one with Jesus as he and the Father are one. "Delight yourself in the Lord, and he will give you the desires of your heart" (Psalm 37:4). Who are we to tell God that we know what's best for us? That we are well aware of what we need, when we need it, how much of it we need, and why we require it?

God's plans are so driven toward salvation that even death can be used to save someone. We are to work with God and not against him; it is when we work with him that he acts on our behalf. "And this is the confidence that we have toward him, that if we ask anything according to his will he hears us. And if we know that he hears us in whatever we ask, we know that we have the requests that we have asked of him" (John 5:14–15).

Psalm 37 is not suggesting that we are not to have desires of our own, but rather that we should desire what God desires for us, being created for his purpose. When we are in accord with God and moving along his paved path, then we are seeking to obtain God's will for us. Our hearts will be in Christ at that point, and we will desire only what is best for us through our Father's eyes.

Uncovering what is delightful and pleasing to our Creator is more simple than difficult. The Bible gives plenty of direction. Our Father desires for us to be like Jesus: "Have this mind among yourselves, which is yours in Christ Jesus" (Philippians 2:5). He wants us to be filled with the Holy Spirit and its fruit (Galatians 5:22–23). He wants us to intercede on behalf of everyone (1 Timothy 2:1), while trusting him through prayer (1 Thessalonians 5:17). We should seek the lost so they may be saved (Matthew 18:10–14) and search Scripture, familiarizing ourselves with his ways and promises (Acts 17:11; Joshua 1:6–9). We should encourage one another and be one while working together day after day (Hebrews 3:13). We should grow stronger spiritually (1 Peter 2:2), and remove our hands from the issues of this life, placing them instead in God's hand (1 Peter 5:7).

Most importantly, God is pure love. He desires love more than anything (Hosea 6:6; Matthew 9:13). If surrendering is how we obtain Jesus's characteristics, then love completes the exchange. Love fastens together everything (Colossians 3:14).

These are but a few examples of what God wills for us and definitely should be in our prayers.

After reading closely the stories of a few characters in the Bible, I imagined being in their distress. I focused on what made them pray so that I might find out exactly why they promoted prayer. Their rationale for prayer was that it connected them with their Father in the best way they could achieve.

For instance, there is Abram (later Abraham). For him, prayer gave proof that the Lord had shown, did show, and would show Abram favor (Genesis 15:6). Realizing this, Abram allowed God to do as he said, and Abram received God's promises without lifting his hand in his own power, in some cases.

Hannah, Samuel's mother, defined prayer as an escape from the fortification of worldly grief (1 Samuel 1). Prayer removed sorrow and created a void of trust, allowing hope to inhabit that once desolate place. Prayer was a loss of trust in oneself, and in man for that matter, and building faith in the Father. Hannah simply poured out all of the cares that filled her cup of anxiety, knowing that God not only heard her, but that he was very concerned as well.

King David, the man after God's own heart, understood prayer as humbling oneself in the Lord. Prayer is an acknowledgment that our Father is the God of standards and rules, the God of the purpose we are to serve. He would tell me that the very secrets of God are shown through prayer, secrets that ignorance does not reveal to us, such as salvation and the Spirit of Truth. For David, receiving and acknowledging God's love occurs through our requests. Prayer is the intersection of God's plan and man's petitions. Once this confluence occurs, man flows along the path of God's purpose instead of continuing in a purely human direction.

King Hezekiah would plead that prayer is the child in distress, troubled over simple cares brought by day-to-day tragedy. We are to call out to the helper of helpers with our pains. In turn we will receive the joy of comfort that comes from trusting the Creator. We know through prayer that God is always at work, always steadfast in mercy and grace. God is willing to provide and fulfill the duties of the loving parent that he is to us all. Prayer is the speech of obedience and brings the reward of God's grace.

Jesus, all knowing, all loving, shows us that prayer is the obedient lesson we bring to ourselves so that God may lift us up to him. Prayer is purest when we are submissive (2 Samuel 7:14; Hebrews 1:5). It is more than spoken words, more than the thought of sending petitions, and absolutely never sacrificial. Prayer is the mind knowing that there is a will beyond our own, the heart choosing to commune with God to be a part of his purpose. Prayer is how God protects us, how he comforts us, how he works in our lives, and how miracles are presented to us. Jesus testifies that the life found in prayer provides the very air that God's children need to breathe in a sinful atmosphere. It's a vital part of our circle of life.

Prayer should precede and succeed decisions and actions. Our Father, unlike our earthly parents, cares about everything we are faced with. "Do not be anxious about anything, but in everything by prayer and supplication with thanksgiving let your request be made known to God" (Philippians 4:6). Being created in God's image gives us a prerequisite to accompany him. Prayer grants us the ability to see God's power; our prayers alone are to glorify God completely by being in accord with his will (1 John 5:14–15).

I believe that prayer is currency of the highest value. Having a blessing and God's favor in our lives requires payment that only this currency can satisfy. Only authentic payments make it through; counterfeits aren't accepted. True currency is created from the purest of faith. How much we accrue and expend depends solely upon the amount of personal treasure we commit. Rest assured that there will never be a "Closed," "Out of Stock," or "Out of Business" sign on God's door. This currency has everlasting value and acceptance.

Luke chapter 11 begins with Jesus praying in a "certain place," and his disciples ask to teach them to pray. Jesus uses a story to illustrate a powerful emphasis on what I call "petition quantity." "Yet because of his impudence he will rise and give him whatever he needs. And I tell you, ask, and it will be given to you" (Luke 11:8–9). If I were to ask for something and be denied once, how would the denier understand how dire my need was? Inconsistency would show that my petition was not as important as it seemed.

God knows our hearts, according to 1 Samuel 16:9, but he does not take it upon himself to do what we need if we do not have faith in asking. Our hearts must show that we are seeking God and what is promised to us; being persistent is how we present our faith. "But the righteous shall live by their faithfulness to God" (Habakkuk 2:4; Romans 1:17). Merely asking God for a petition does not absolutely indicate our fervent need regarding that petition. World peace would be great, but if we prayed for that, would we really, honestly want it? If so, how badly would we want it? Would it be enough to request it day and night endlessly, interceding on behalf of those figures that could make it happen?

Thankfully, we know not to pray for that (Matthew 10:34). But in the same way, God wants a loving, willing heart of prayer that does not suggest the prayer as a sacrifice of one's time. On the contrary, petition quantity influences acceptance that divinity should have ultimate control. Often times it's simple to pray while misplacing one's position with God's place in answers to prayer.

Our enemy is remarkably swift and clever. He hits us with the boldest and most compromising attacks. At times we do not even realize we are being harassed. So how do we fight an adversary that we cannot defeat?

Prayer is the answer. Our flesh turns against us at every moment, and we move right along with it at times. But the power of God's Holy Spirit fends off the tactics of the enemy. Satan's tactics go beyond our ability because of his authority in the atmosphere (Ephesians 2:2). But with God all things are possible; anything can be handled through his aid.

The facts suggest that since no one can fight for himself (because we will fall every time), our biggest enemy is us. Jesus's trust in God enabled his battle with Satan to be won through knowing and applying God's Word exactly where the attacks hit. Filled with the Holy Spirit, Jesus used his faith in God to obtain victory. He did not trust in himself or his desires (Matthew 4:1–11, 26:39).

Prayer for the power of the Holy Spirit is the most effective prayer that we can kneel down and request. Those who pray this prayer ought to understand what will take place when the Holy Spirit comes. The Spirit of Truth is a force so powerful that the prayer to be prepared to receive God's Spirit should both precede and succeed the prayer for the Spirit itself. The Spirit brings wisdom, conviction, and boldness—fruitful characteristics that all work together. Most of all, once we have removed ourselves so that we can do God's will and fulfill his purpose, we can only be stopped by our choosing.

The prayer for the Spirit clothes us in the same righteousness as Christ and organizes us to work for our own and others' salvation. Prayer is the most effective, knowledgeable, and reasonable way to live a life for Christ. Without it, the enemy tallies up another score in the "attack" column, driving us further from God's endless contributions. As long as Jesus has not come back to take his flock into the kingdom, there will be a need for prayer.

Chapter 4

Presents from the Past

Being healed from the past is one of the greatest feelings, testimonies, and faith builders that God's grace will allow. God is patiently waiting to use us for his glory, and we are our own biggest enemies when we don't allow him to do that. Travel light by releasing the baggage and you are mobile to go further. That's what being healed is all about.

We may be carrying a great deal of hurt caused by accusers in our past. The best hope we have to look forward to—other than never dealing with the offender again—is knowing that emotional pain can heal just as well as physical pain. When we make the choice to have restoration, the healing is more effective. When and only when we are ready to heal, we should approach it at a pace that is comfortable. The time it takes to rebuild one's character depends solely on the individual. When someone is not familiar with the healing process, then the hurt is more likely to become uncontrolled. Other stressors can activate the old pain. It takes more than an "I'm sorry" and a few pages of calendar to repair the damage.

Any and all negative emotions are completely normal; there is no issue in that. The problem lies in not dealing with those feelings. If neglected, they can draw us deeper into the web of hurt. We may even trap others in that web. We may engage in a causality that states, "I am hurt, so I inflict hurt." One example of this is passive aggression. Passive aggression does not confront the true problem because the victim is typically someone other than the offender.

Something else we should know about feelings is that, although negative emotions are normal, we nevertheless must remove these emotions so that the hurt inside of us will end. If we don't take care of those feelings, then the hurt will reappear, even if we have no understanding of why it is that we continue feeling it.

The best way for us to move along in the healing process is to talk about whatever trauma we have faced. We must find the most qualified person to communicate with up to the point of completion, which is acceptance. Holding anything inside is the biggest foolery we fall for. We aren't holding it; it's really holding us. It holds us back from everything that would reveal it as a disadvantage. It burdens our ability to live a full life. When trauma holds us, we give offenders the authority to continue their oppression through the negative feelings we have toward them.

There is hope, however. Through time, effort, patience, and acceptance, we will be released from the burden of any pain.

IDENTIFY

Identify what you're going through. For instance, say you've identified anger as the emotion you're feeling, and you recognize that it isn't rational—you may go into a rage at any moment, whether it's over a minute issue or a colossal disturbance. You can deal with this anger better after you have gained a broader understanding about anger.

It's completely normal to feel anger; we were made with this emotion. Nothing in this world will be endlessly pleasant. It's natural that anger will surface. The question is what happens after the anger? How long should you feel angry?

Psalm 4:4 reads, "Be angry, and do not sin; ponder in your own hearts on your beds, and be silent. Offer right sacrifices, and put your trust in the Lord." There's a similar text in Ephesians 4:26: "Be angry and do not sin; do not let the sun go down on your anger."

We are fine when we get angry because, like compassion, anger urges us into a reaction. However, that reaction should lead us to God and his will. Experiencing anger and holding on to it causes our minds to warp around whatever caused it. This can send hate and revenge into our hearts, which gives opportunity to our flesh and the enemy. "Beloved, never avenge yourselves, but leave it to the wrath of God, for it is written: 'Vengeance is mine, I will repay, says the Lord'" (Romans 12:19; see also Deuteronomy 32:35).

Maybe what you are feeling is not anger at all, but hurt. Hurt can lure us into sheltering ourselves away from everything that we can. We may weep unexpectedly when something triggers the remembrance of our pain. Mind and body can become intimate with hurt, making us one with it. Then we'll fail ourselves in many ways. We'll fail at loving, fail at caring, fail at the sense of self-worth. We'll cease to notice our own achievements. Hurt can even cause us to blame ourselves for the pain. This kind of heartbreak has no benefits whatsoever. No one can be his/herself while hurting. One reason is because there is no sense of happiness forming around him. Without happiness, joy is far off.

It can be easy for someone else to say, "Let go!" Yes, in a sense it really is as easy as "letting go," but we are not pre-equipped to "let go" of something we did not choose to grab hold of in the first place.

Think of an uncontrolled emotion as a car that is moving with you in the driver's seat. You could easily let go of the steering wheel, but what then? Is this car going to drive itself? What you need is to find a way to get out of the driver's seat. Then, once the ride is over, you can walk away from it.

The reason we don't stop the car ourselves is because if we could, then our feelings wouldn't be taking us for a ride in the first place. We need someone else to rely on who understands how to control these emotions without being overtaken by them. That someone must have the credibility that comes from experience, an experience that supersedes our own. "Humble yourselves, therefore, under the mighty hand of God so that at the proper time he may exalt you, casting all your anxieties on him, because he cares for you" (1 Peter 5:6-7).

"So that's it?" you may be wondering. As simple as it sounds, yes, that's it.

> The Lord is a stronghold for the oppressed, a stronghold in times of trouble. (Psalm 9:9)

> The name of the Lord is a strong tower; the righteous man runs into it and is safe. (Proverbs 18:10)

> [Jesus] was despised and rejected by men; a man of sorrows, and acquainted with grief. (Isaiah 53:3)

Jesus continued in that grief to death and conquered it all. This gives him credibility and reliability to handle whatever we go through when we are sorrowful.

THE TRUTH

One question that may surface is, "What if I cannot get things right with God?" Or even, "What if I do not know how to reach him?"

These are bumps in the road, obstacles that may make us consider changing our minds, but no one ever made it to the finish line without some type of challenge. Usain Bolt, the fastest man alive, still had to beat several competitors in order to win his races. His titles weren't handed to him because of his reputation.

We aren't going to get our healing, our win, our victory, just out of pity for the fact we have lost so often. True, "He regards the prayer of the destitute and does not despise their prayer" (Psalm 102:17). God wants us to trust him. The Holy Bible is full of instances in which he pleads with people to stop what they're doing in their own strength, failing at every turn, and to place trust in him.

Another question is, "Why trust God if he knows everything and the hurt that happened to me was allowed?" That is an honest question. Taking what we know and applying it will lead to the understanding that this world is ruled by sinful nature. We are given a choice: we can choose to obey or to disobey. The consequences of our choices travel through ages and generations. We learn and act as those before us have done, and pick up many other traits along the way.

"Everyone who makes a practice of sinning also practices lawlessness; sin is lawlessness" (1 John 3:4). Whoever decides to burden, pain, or traumatize us in any way has done so by choice. They choose to do wrong. God won't force himself on anyone. This is why you, someone who strives to act correctly, still have struggles within yourself. You and I won't do what is morally correct under God if we do not submit to him by putting off our self-centered desires.

That said, God longs for us to endure the sufferings of this world so that, in return, we are strengthened like gold refined by fire. Understanding suffering, we are not only prepared to be in a place that brings peace (Isaiah 26:3), but also prepared to live where we will never have to deal with sinful nature again.

"He will make a complete end; trouble will not rise up a second time" (Nahum 1:9). In our struggles and times of affliction, we aren't meant to be overwhelmed. God weighs everything and knows that we can make it through these difficult episodes. "No temptation is uncommon to man. God is faithful, and he will not let you be tempted beyond your ability, but with the temptation he will also provide the way of escape, that you may be able to endure it" (1 Corinthians 10:13). This text applies to us as well as our offenders. Yes, there is a way to escape the desire to hurt others. But if we don't trust God when he says that way is there, we'll travel down another path that may lead to life-changing consequences.

Even Jesus, the Son of Man and Son of God, had to endure the pain and suffering this world offers. He did it all by choice so that he could be our example. He wants us, too, to depend solely on God our Father and make it through. "Take my yoke upon you and learn from me, for I am gentle and lowly in heart, and you will find rest for your souls. For my yoke is easy, and my burden is light" (Matthew 11:28–30).

Jesus knew firsthand that this life is not promised to be easy or smooth. He kept pressing toward his goal because of the magnitude of what finishing the race means. There was something bigger than him and his problems. Our lives and the salvation that we are able to accept are of higher value than the mockery that he suffered.

Firm belief that God will perform in your life will enable you to persevere through any challenge. "And the peace of God, which surpasses all understanding, will guard your hearts and your minds in Christ Jesus" (Philippians 4:7). Paul also tells us not to be anxious for anything, but at all times, in every situation, to lift up prayers to God with thanksgiving.

I promise you that we can trust God to take that steering wheel of our emotions and bring order so that we may begin to have a fulfilled life.

TIME TO CHOOSE

The hurt may still be challenging to think about, and even harder to get over. The idea of it can be as potent as poison. What occurred in the past may have the ability to rot our thoughts in the present, causing us to wither emotionally.

In our effort to be healed, however, this is part of the process. Don't aspire to get past the event miraculously and never remember any details. When you're ready, the achievement is moving on with your life—being yourself again, mentally.

Whoever your accuser was, he or she was not in the correct state of mind morally. According to Romans 8:7–8, "For the mind that is set on the flesh is hostile to God, for it does not submit to God's law; indeed it cannot. Those who are in the flesh cannot please God." My point is not to excuse an accuser's behavior in any way. Nor am I implying that we should accept behavior that is hostile due to ignorance of what is greater.

In order for us to cease hurting inside and move toward complete healing, we have to forgive any individuals who are holding us back, mentally and emotionally. This is true even if they don't ask for our forgiveness. The purpose of our forgiveness is not for them, but for ourselves. Freedom from hurt, oppression, pain, and sorrow lies in our forgiveness. Without forgiveness, we are controlled by our emotions. Through forgiveness, we sleep peacefully and rise with the joy that God granted us in our hearts. We aren't to hold others to blame because blame leads to resentment, which can affect those who have committed no wrong against us. Forgiveness is in no way forgetting; forgetting may never come.

God not only wants us to forgive, but he is also ready and willing to forgive also. "If we confess our sins, he is faithful and just to forgive us our sins, and cleanse us from all unrighteousness" (John 1:9). God grants us the heart willing to forgive, because without it and without him, forgiveness is unsuccessful. This even means that if the offender requested forgiveness for wrongs committed with a sincere heart, God has definitely forgave and will not hold remembrance of the offense.

As I stated before, we are stronger through the experiences that we endure, and part of that strength is for someone else's benefit. "[God] comforts us in all our affliction, so that we may be able to comfort those who are in any affliction, with the comfort with which we ourselves are comforted by God. For as we share abundantly in Christ's sufferings, so through Christ we share abundantly in comfort too" (2 Corinthians 1:4–5). Place your all in God, and he will grant all that he offers in his Word. God would love for you to take him at his Word, because in that he receives the glory and you receive the victory. "More than that, we rejoice in our sufferings, knowing that suffering produces endurance, and endurance produces character, and character produces hope, and hope does not put us to shame, because God's love has been poured into our hearts through the Holy Spirit who has been given to us" (Romans 5:3–5).

The road will be difficult, but remember that God is already getting you past it. The result is completely dependent upon what we choose. We have to trust God in order to accept his help; otherwise we are lost.

CHAPTER 5

"Abstain from All Appearance of Evil"

*Look at Mary Magdalene's story. During their first meeting, Jesus said
to sin no more (John 8). As Mary anointed Jesus's feet, she was told that
her sins were forgiven and to go in peace (Luke 7). Mary gave away
a great number of her possessions to acquire the box of fragrances, and
we know that it is only after we repent that we faithfully value Christ.
Then, we are willing to offer and release anything for our Lord.*

Take someone with a self-made initiative, remove their drive, divide the instinct in half, multiply it by humility and abnegation, and then add ascription that only God can provide. The recipe may puzzle an average mind, but the formula makes for only a single outcome: self-control. It's what binds every other perfect attribute that makes up holiness.

We strive to apply this adhesive to our lives. We'll place it directly in our cores so that we'll maintain control through any circumstances. Many times self-control is not recognized for what it is because it's called something else—willpower, for example. If self-control is an operating system, similar to a computer (a system based upon numerous applications that runs the hardware it's applied to), then willpower is the factory-set calculator—very insignificant. Self-control's complexity is that it isn't restraint or abstention from a few attractions, pleasures, or temptations. It is restraint every time from every one of them.

Now it's true that everyone isn't enticed by the same things. For some, self-control may not seem applicable to behaviors like stealing, lying, or covetousness. Even if one does not feel the temptation, the fact is that self-control indeed governs one from falling into those snares.

However, one natural exercise that is permissible exclusively, in general should be excluded because it holds a universal effect: sexual conduct. Sex is an act that can be a prelude to something a lot bigger. Some outcomes can cause one's reality to appear repulsive and unacceptable, like homosexuality, pedophilia, and rape. Then there is behavior that may seem common, like promiscuity. We fall into these traps once we are exposed to sex.

The purpose of placing stipulations on sexual conduct is for all to uphold and encourage premarital abstinence, because the internal effects of sexual activity aren't avoidable. Sadly, many people are comfortable being sexually active apart from a spouse, which explains why there are few who turn away.

GOD'S GIFT

After creation, according to Genesis chapter 1, the command that God gave the first divinely established human relationship was to be fruitful and multiply. Today's translation is simple—have fun and have kids. Sex, in its plentiful ways, is only true when given to only one true other. Sex offers, excites, and gratifies in such an exclusive way that it can't be compared to anything else. The connection that two individuals share before, during, and after being fruitful is better than any therapy, group activity, agreement, or gift that the two can experience because of what goes on within them both. Minds and bodies connect on many levels before touching so that bodies will come together and fulfill each other's inborn desires.

Just sit back and think about all that goes on. Take the parameters of attraction, including the feeling that it brings. It starts by noticing an attractive person and then the realization of their mutual fondness, which sets the stage for the affection two individuals share.

Males are born to have bodies that attract females and vice versa. God made it so, just as he made other things so, like teaching, reproving, and following correct standards for living. The pursuit for another's affection should lead to a long list of things and then ultimately sex—in that order. Immaturity doesn't appreciate this gift, and infidelity will never fathom that it is a gift. God gave the gift and will bring the prize to every one of his believers. Everything that causes one to crave premature sexual attention is unacceptable and should be filtered from one's lifestyle.

The fact is, everyone is not *doing it*. I have met individuals in their late twenties, even in their forties, who have made it without succumbing to the social pressure to engage in premarital sex. It is like any choice that expresses a cherished standard. For example, I have always abstained from smoking. I valued my lungs because I am an athlete. I have never met someone that I believed I couldn't match up with. So—in my head—I am one of the greatest athletes to ever walk the earth (I don't box, so I can't send that message to Floyd). Healthy lungs are something I cherish as part of my identity. They are a positive, productive achievement.

The possibilities are bright when it comes to being abstinent. It's all in what one does rather than what one doesn't do.

Neurological Control

The hidden matter is in the biochemistry of attraction and sexual behavior. Understanding what goes on in this process will better explain the reason why we choose who we choose and what we choose, and even why we regularly have trouble fighting it off. Because of biochemistry's neurological control, sex, in my opinion, is as much a form of substance abuse as are alcohol and drug addictions.

What drives humans is an endogenous neurotransmitter (an innate brain communicator) called *dopamine*. Dopamine triggers many functions, including desires and urges, which connect it with addictions. In her book *Dirty Minds: How Our Brains Influence Love, Sex, and Relationships*, Kayt Sukel tackles the complexities in attraction and arousal, as well as the benefits and misfortunes that result from our brain activities. "When you look closer at the behavioral effects resulting from too much or too little dopamine in the basal ganglia, you can see why . . . it must underlie the neurobiology of love," says Kayt.[1]

The science explains that once we experience arousal or pleasure in something, sexual behavior in this case, our brains are signaled to produce high levels of dopamine. If the experience wasn't pleasing, then dopamine isn't released, telling the brain the effort wasn't worth it.

Dopamine reactions aren't exclusive to sex. Noticeable levels are released during plenty of activities like eating chocolate, shopping,

---

[1]   Kayt Sukel, *Dirty Minds: How Our Brains Influence Love, Sex, and Relationships* (New York: The Free Press, 2012), 44.

"cuddling with your kids, holding hands with your significant other," and so on.[2] In the case of displaying affection, that could cause one to seek greater levels of pleasure. From sharing smiles, to holding hands, to holding one another, to kissing is a progressive heightening of arousal. That tells the brain that's where the bar is set, so accept nothing less than the most recent level of pleasure. Some people feel as if they go nuts until that level is achieved.

Sexual behavior makes a high impact because the high levels of dopamine it produces encourages one to regular sexual conduct. One's brain chemistry creates sexually driven thoughts. The brain adjusts to a given level of dopamine and works in favor of those thoughts. Resisting temptation seems futile because the body (carnal desire) is working against the conscious mind's intention to refrain from sex.

There is another important brain chemical called *oxytocin*. "[The hypothalamus] area has a say on which hormones, those great behavioral primers, are released into the bloodstream and into the brain . . . Oxytocin is a bit of a wonder compound . . . In response to touch, sex, and social bonds, oxytocin stimulates cells . . . Once stimulated, these cells then initiate that lovely and agreeable dopamine cascade in the basal ganglia."[3]

In other words, oxytocin is responsible for creating a connection with someone or something else. This pair-bonding chemical will create emotional ties between those who experience deep sexual arousal with one another. When oxytocin and dopamine work side by side, they create the potential for the brain to crave sex spontaneously.

So say a person takes part in a sexual act, and a union is created between that person and the person's partner. The brain is on board and the body is fulfilled. If the original partner then isn't present, those high dopamine levels can influence the person's behavior, urging him to find a new partner to achieve another

---

[2]   Sukel, *Dirty Minds*, 47.
[3]   Sukel, *Dirty Minds*, 48–49.

dopamine high. That desperate person is only one decision away from falling into promiscuity.

That's only one of many scenarios demonstrating the dangers of premarital relations and immature thinking that lead to reckless or uncontrolled decisions.

To say that the mind and body are always "on" for sex is incorrect. There is an off-season controlled by the mood-manager chemical *serotonin*. When dopamine levels rise, serotonin levels decrease, and vice versa. Serotonin is often referred to as a brake, a way to stanch the dopamine flood so you aren't always in thrall to those good feelings.[4]

There is another chemical called *prolactin*. It is released once an orgasm is achieved. It eases the mind to stop the passion for sex, but only temporarily. The libido will eventually build sexual craving again.

Though serotonin and prolactin ease dopamine withdrawal, abstinence is superior to the body's natural method to fight off a craving. Without the sexual experience (thoughts, images, conversations, and acts) prompting high dopamine levels, we will not have much of a fight to put up with. If one has taken part in carnal behavior, replacing those experiences with completely different activities enables the mind to shift away from the established chemical processes. An idle mind may more easily pick up bad old habits than a mind that is occupied and moving in a different direction.

THE GOSPEL TRUTH

The apostle Paul, in 1 Thessalonians 5:22, tells us to "abstain from all appearance of evil."

Having sex is not evil; God ordained intercourse as a gift to a husband and his wife. "Therefore a man shall leave his father and

---

4   Sukel, *Dirty Minds*, 53.

his mother and hold fast to his wife, and they shall become one flesh" (Genesis 2:24).

Fornication, adultery, and sexual immorality cause sex to become evil—evil because of what this kind of sex represents outside of its purpose. Sex is like hunger. It is not an emotion that goes away, but a drive that must be fulfilled. When that drive is directed outside of its purpose, it goes against the Spirit's fruit. It becomes a purely fleshy desire that people fight daily. "For I know that nothing good dwells in me, that is, in my flesh. For I have the desire to do what is right, but not the ability to carry it out. For I do not do the good I want, but the evil I do not want is what I keep on doing" (Romans 7:18–19).

God's Word has all the ammunition that we need to defend ourselves, but if we are not educated concerning our arsenal, the fight won't last long nor go in our favor.

Naively, we may believe we can simply say a rational "No!" However, dopamine is persuasive. The fight is not as easy as it seems on the surface. Imagine you have grown up eating cheeseburgers at home. For an experiment, you stop eating cheeseburgers once you move to your own apartment. Then an invitation arrives to attend a family barbecue.

While you are there, the most tempting grilled sensation is waved under your nose. The smell acts like an attractive pheromone. Probably you haven't eaten all day. To top it off, everyone around you is enjoying a similar burger. They entice you to join them, telling you how great it tastes.

The point is that the mind directs us. It knows what we need and what we crave. It places us in the position to accept those cravings. Since the brain is this powerful, it's clear why the Word of God encourages self-control and a higher way of thinking. "Do not be conformed to this world, but be transformed by the renewal of your mind, that by testing you may discern what is the will of God, what is good and acceptable and perfect" (Romans 12:2).

DEFINITE DEFIANCE

Abstinence could be explained as holding oneself back voluntarily, especially from something regarded as improper or unhealthy. Because sexual immorality is ungodly behavior (see Acts 15:20), then abstinence means drawing closer to God in Christlike behavior. "Submit yourselves therefore to God. Resist the devil, and he will flee from you. Draw near to God, and he will draw near to you" (James 4:7–8).

Our bodies are temples of the Holy Spirit; we in no way belong to ourselves. The price of sin is too high for us to pay; therefore Jesus became our substitute. If our bodies were sacrificed in place of Christ's body, could we be raised in our death? Would we be able to pay our own wage for sin? (See 1 Corinthians 6:19–20.) No; we are definitely not our own. We have been created in an image that is not ours (Genesis 1:26–27).

The word that says it all in the definition is *voluntarily*. Our choices and actions shows exactly what we are about. "The good person out of the good treasure of his heart produces good, and the evil person out of his evil treasure produces evil, for out of the abundance of the heart his mouth speaks" (Luke 6:45).

The choice to follow Christ has to be sure and sincere for there to be a true mind-set focused on abstinence. The carnal mind will directly oppose what is holy. Our help is not in and of ourselves; we can only make the choice to accept God's help. Praying in the Spirit and for the Spirit renews our strength, giving us sound, guilt-free psyche.

Philippians 2:1–5 describes how our brains should function in order for us to completely abide in Christ:

> So if there is any encouragement in Christ, any comfort from love, any participation in the Spirit, any affection and sympathy, complete my joy by being of the same mind, having the same love, being in full accord and of one mind. Do nothing from selfish ambition or conceit, but in humility count others

more significant than yourselves. Let each of you look
not only to his own interests, but also to the interests
of others. Have this mind among yourselves, which is
yours in Christ Jesus.

This again shows that we are to have a higher way of thinking,
being renewed in our minds. This is acquiring the mind-set of
Christ. Tuned in with Christ's mind, our thoughts are at ease.

Concerning sex, "As long as I'm not having sex, I'm fine"
is a carnal mind-set. The mind in the Spirit abstains from
contemplation of sexual touching, gestures, thoughts, and verbal
and optical signs. There is no gravitation toward crude, explicit,
uncouth, or vulgar behavior.

WORTH THE WAIT

Abstaining from intercourse until marriage prevents plenty of
harms. We can rule out the danger of sexual activity controlling
our way of thinking, thus avoiding what I like to call "the itch,
cough, soothe effect." We know now that dopamine causes desires
(the "itch"). Therefore we are forced to react (the "cough"). Then
we search for pleasure (the "soothe"). The result is only temporary
satisfaction, leading to the next itch. Abstinence short-circuits this
effect.

The main objective in following Christ is protection. Jesus
is our protector; his words of wisdom protect us from inheriting
the death that everyone deserves (see Romans 5:12). In a more
immediate sense, we are free from instant harm as well. "The body
is not meant for sexual immorality, but for the Lord, and the Lord
for the body . . . Flee from sexual immorality. Every other sin a
person commits is outside the body, but the sexually immoral
person sins against his own body" (1 Corinthians 6:13, 6:18).
Because sexual immorality defiles us, we not only put our body
in harm's way concerning unrighteousness, but also concerning
physical impairments and abnormalities.

Indulging in sexual conduct threatens our health and raises our chances of contracting sexually transmitted diseases. Contraceptives mitigate some of this risk, but they are not risk-free either. The pill, the morning-after pill, the patch, and the shot can cause deficiency in other areas for women. The risks are magnified when contraceptives are used repeatedly. Even a condom has risk. The Bible speaks on sexual immorality in more than ten books. It would be sad to suffer the trauma of this world and then also fall into judgment for actively defiling oneself. We will choose correctly because of the value we place on God and his law. As David wrote in Psalm 40:8, "I delight to do your will, O my God; your law is within my heart."

Intercourse is solely for married couples. Because of affection, neurological effects, and the physical risks of early sexual behavior and exposure, sex does not belong among the activities of minors or even single young adults.

Sex is meant for marriage for a reason. If we are to live long and prosperous lives, why then would we, at a young age and in our days of learning, choose to act in this way? Comprehension of the seriousness of sex should lead us to comply with lessons of safety and understand exactly what lies behind the face of sinful desire. God warned us about the sinful aspects of sex long ago; we have the opportunity to make an informed choice before falling victim to postsexual mental and physical suffering. There shouldn't be a trial-and-error sequence in following God's law and order. Unfortunately, trial and error often accompanies an imperfect being's way of life.

"For this is the will of God, your sanctification: that you abstain from sexual immorality; that each one of you know how to control his own body in holiness and honor, not in the passion of lust . . ." (1 Thessalonians 4:3–5).

CHAPTER 6

Salvation: Under Construction

There is absolutely nothing more beautiful than salvation, than watching someone who held allegiance to the world surrender selfish desires, boldly forfeiting his life to God, the Creator of heaven and earth. What does it take for someone to have that freedom of salvation? What is behind the scenes on our road to recovery?

Universal void is obsolete. Temporal nightfall and frequent light are in its place. Waters rush and are forced upon solid surfaces. Land is marked and the new sky transports the sea-breeze aroma to every fruit-yielding and seed-bearing plant. The breath inhaled by a living creature fills the lungs, pure and delicate, encouraging the next breath. The sky's endless brilliance calms the burn of the novel sun. Several evenings and mornings later, man's kingdom now reigns. The ruler of earth makes his presence known to the rest of creation. As a reward for his diligence, the Creator grants him not only dominion, but a helper. An equal, another soul to unite with and contribute to while his days elapse. "She shall be called Woman" (Genesis 2:23).

Instantly drawn to her, man strengthens their bond by manifesting their flesh as one. They are never to be apart or alone.

But a fresh ruler would soon draw his eyes away from the everlasting to an amusement that satisfied his five senses: his wife, the pinnacle of arousal for an audience of one. Once Adam crossed the line between admiration and adoration, the trap was set and the test was at hand.

"You will not surely die. For God knows that when you eat of it your eyes will be opened, and you will be like God, knowing good and evil" (Genesis 3:4–5).

Accepting the fruit from his loved one indicated that Adam regarded Eve as first and God second. Adam ignored his Lord's will and applied worship to the creation rather than the Creator. The precept of obedience in a relationship with God was disregarded.

Man exercised that mystery, free will, and the results were evident. He became naked and ashamed. The need to cover up for the first time indicated that man and woman were strangers in their own home. Unknown abilities began to give way to their unnatural state.

As the day drew near sunset, the evening wind made its way into the primitive kingdom. The Lord God, Father of all creation, descended from heaven to commune with man and woman, as was his custom. However, Adam and Eve were not logically organized to take part in this customary service. Speechless and confused, their disorientation signaled their lost state. This was the first time these two had been unsure. They simply did not have the necessary knowledge to cope with being fallen. The priest of the home exclaimed to his Lord, "I heard the sound of you in the garden, and I was afraid, because I was naked, and I hid myself" (Genesis 3:10).

For Adam to fear the Lord in such a way, fueled by terror, was an unbelievably profound observation.

"Who told you that you were naked?" (Genesis 3:11).

The Lord's reply suggests that he was flabbergasted at this finding. This was a scheduled event, a time agreed, so to speak, during which Creator and creation would intimately come together and take part in each other's lives. Their bond was strengthened during this time of day. Things were obviously different now. What had caused Adam to lose his first love, and why was there fear in place of welcoming comfort?

Adam and Eve had been created with a special substance that gave them connection to God. Now not so much. It was as if it had never existed. "Then the eyes of both were opened, and they knew they were naked" (Genesis 3:7).

The deceiver had explained that Eve would be like God, knowing good and evil, but obedience of God's commands rules out what is evil to the Lord. Man did not need to know good and evil, but maybe sought to practice good and evil. Even the man's efforts to cleave to his wife were in vain. He no longer led her when she freely ate of the tree, nor was he fully united with her when he explained, "The woman whom you gave to be with me, she gave me fruit of the tree, and I ate" (Genesis 3:12). Finagled by the deceiver, Adam stood alone momentarily. He strayed from his Lord's side, yet could not fully stand firm at his wife's side.

When disobedience opened their eyes, their first thought was to conceal themselves—but why? Was there someone or something to hide from or make their appearance presentable for? Making garments was useless because the acts they were trying to cover needed a better outcome altogether. Their leaf garments were replaced with skin garments from the Lord God, revealing that their actions to fix what they had broken were insufficient. The

Lord was the only one who could place upon them an acceptable covering.

To regain the substance they had lost, allowing Creator and creation to freely fellowship face-to-face, called for a design. No longer did man have a paved trail to walk to God. Rather, a stony, breathtaking mountain had to be climbed and conquered. The plan of salvation had commenced. The first sacrifice proved that the works of men and their disputes were useless.

"And the dragon and his angels fought back, but he was defeated, and there was no longer any place for them in heaven. And the great dragon was thrown down, that ancient serpent, who is called the devil and Satan, the deceiver of the whole world—he was thrown down to the earth, and his angels were thrown down with him" (Revelation 12:7–9).

The earth suffered infiltration, and the inhabitants were unprepared to defend their home. Ignorant of the war, man's battle on the spiritual level proved catastrophic. The two casualties forfeited their reign, kingdom, and home. The throne of the world gave way to an age of spiritual slavery. Bound in chains and destined to die, mankind's unworthy option was to give in, as most of them did. The fall of the two ancestors in their garden dwelling gave the enemy a helping hand in his war for control: flesh, mankind's own desires. The very things carnal nature required would lead to constant struggle and fall.

"I will put enmity between you and the woman, and between your offspring and her offspring; he shall bruise your head, and you shall bruise his heel" (Genesis 3:15).

Creation was almost helpless against the enemy's schemes and attacks. The devourer hastened to destroy these sitting ducks. Adam, crafted by the Lord's very hands, stumbled over his desire and fell captive to transgression. Was the enemy lucky or tactful? A predator perhaps, as he stalked and studied his prey, waiting for a point of vulnerability to pounce.

You were the signet of perfection, full of wisdom
and perfect in beauty. You were in Eden, the garden of

God; every precious stone was your covering . . . and
crafted in gold were your settings and your engravings.
On the day that you were created they were prepared.
You were anointed guardian cherub. I placed you;
you were on the holy mountain of God . . . You were
blameless in your ways from the day you were created,
till unrighteousness was found in you. In the abundance
of your trade you were filled with violence in your
midst, and you sinned; so I cast you as a profane thing
from the mountain of God . . . Your heart was proud
because of your beauty; you corrupted your wisdom
for the sake of your splendor. I cast you to the ground;
I exposed you before kings, to feast their eyes on you.
(Ezekiel 28:12–17)

The knowledge of good and evil, when presented to Earth's
foe, took him just as it took Earth's first ruler at his test. The fallen
angel chose his fate, and pride brought his decline. With knowledge
of right and wrong, he chose evil, but he was first created perfect.
Perfection requires knowledge and understanding—wisdom. To
stay perfect, Lucifer would have had to know what iniquity was
and then not yielded to the temptation of transgression.

To stop man from maturing in his own perfection, Satan used
the woman to break the connection that kept Adam in direct
communion with the Lord God. And yes, Adam adored his wife.

Therefore Satan's argument for creation to defy their Creator
(Genesis 3:4) has no justification, similar to the sound of a false
alarm. Mankind has the ability to choose just as the deceiver did,
but Satan's deceptions lure men into choosing to exalt self rather
than give worship, creating for themselves a personal god. On the
contrary; choice does not make one a god, and free will does not
indicate exaltation. Those attributes are confined to the presence
of love. Human choices should be driven by the love inside them,
which is theirs by their freedom of choice. Satan discarded his love
of God and then persuaded man to choose a similar folly. Jealousy

and envy poisoned Cain's love for Abel and caused him to drive his hand against his brother.

"If you do well, will you not be accepted? And if you do not do well, sin is crouching at your door. Its desire is for you, but you must rule over it" (Genesis 4:7).

This lesson, which preceded Cain's act of murder, was impeccable in timing and practicality, keeping watch for lawlessness before the law was given. Evil gained the momentum at this point of the war. Sin took its place in the hearts of the rest of mankind at the beginning of their existence. Transgression would later rise, with the goal of capturing every being. All the men of earth were almost sure to fall and turn against their lord.

> I wait for your salvation, O Lord. (Genesis 49:18)

> Behold, the Lord's hand is not shortened, that it cannot save, or his ear dull, that it cannot hear; but your iniquities have made a separation between you and your God, and your sins have hidden his face from you so that he does not hear. (Isaiah 59:1–2)

The blazing love of the Almighty yearned for intimacy with the people of his pasture. Love like a fire, impossible to extinguish, with a heat that held no temperature, compelled the Shepherd to retrieve the lost back to his fold—if only the sheep would understand his ways. It is a love that gives promises and keeps promises. It is a love that wipes away enemies and chooses to save a people whose desires are far from their loving Maker. However, the movement of one finger was inaugurated, perpetuated, and finalized by the undying, immaculate love that empowers their Lord and often it went unnoticed by those people.

"Your way, O God is in the sanctuary" (Psalm 77:13 NKJV).

And that is where he would be. The sanctuary, assigned to Moses to construct, imported God's presence from heaven to earth. It was a place for Creator and creation to harmonize their fellowship. Mankind worshiped by offering sacrifice, a sacred event not to be mistaken with ritual. Sacrifice was an act for sanctification, a time of repentance, and a prayer for forgiveness by faith. Faith detached the transgression from the sinner, transferring the burden to an animal. When life poured from the animal and the blood was sprinkled, the atonement price was paid for those transgressions.

On the other hand, it was not enough for criminal man to secure his fate merely by killing an unblemished, innocent substitute. There was a meaning in such service, a purpose that extended the experience. Man could not atone for himself, unless of course the leopard had a fair chance of changing its spots. The sanctuary system was a precursor that revealed an ultimate offering that would last indefinitely.

"The old system under the law of Moses was only a shadow, a dim preview of the good things to come, not the good things themselves. The sacrifices under that system were repeated again and again, year after year, but they were never able to provide perfect cleansing for those who came to worship" (Hebrews 10:1 NLT).

The war took a turn. The hearts of men were provided a supplement so they might proceed with a gaze that would stay upon high. The power of the Lord showed strong among mankind. The enemy would no longer maintain the space between them and God. The Lord would transport and supply reinforcement so that none of his people were left without an opportunity to worship. But did God's chosen nation gain morale or would their defeat seem arbitrary?

"O Lord, our Lord, how majestic is your name in all the earth! You have set your glory about the heavens. When I look at your heavens, the work of your fingers, the moon and the stars, which you have set in place, what is man that you are mindful of him, and the son of man that you care for him?" (Psalm 8:1, 8:3–4).

The Lord's compassion toward men makes the most caring mother appear as a neglectful parent, as if love was never affordable to her, causing poverty to spill out in the household. God's faithfulness toward his people suggests that the sun, constantly appearing and shining day after day, is unreliable. God does not encompass even the idea of being unfaithful. When someone appears to hit rock bottom, without a possession to grasp, they have yet to be forgotten by God. God created man. It was not man who assembled the Lord God. Miserably, mankind's representative defiled their relationship. God continues in his quickness to love, care, provide for, sustain, deliver, heal, and protect Adam's offspring.

"Watch and pray that you may not enter into temptation. The spirit indeed is willing, but the flesh is weak" (Matthew 26:41).

No matter how much the Lord gave, some men just would not accept the conceptual purpose of his love.

"For all have sinned and fall short of the glory of God" (Romans 3:23).

Love does not consist of control over a beloved people. Control would rule love out, because love is and comes by the way of choice. The ability to choose is persuaded by one's love. The Almighty identified that once the heart is captured by the goodness that he brings to all the earth, the choice is set. God's love, then bestowed upon the heart, opens the oneness that he intimately desires. All of the characteristics that expound on his mysterious perfection are offered to his people.

"I call heaven and earth to witness against you today, that I have set before you life and death, blessing and curse. Therefore choose life, that you and your offspring may live" (Deuteronomy 30:19).

The road to recovery ends when those on earth who belong to the God of heaven are reunited in paradise. The obstacle is removing the heart disease that sin offerings in the sanctuary could not account for.

"For I desire steadfast love and not sacrifice, the knowledge of God rather than burnt offerings" (Hosea 6:6).

God is excited by faithfulness and acceptant of man's repentance. Sacrifice as ritual, to find a safe zone for the wrong done, was not his intention and will never bring oneness with the Lord. The heart that rejoices in the Lord's works and sings his praises and seeks his righteousness is the heart that exalts his name and stands firm on his Word. This heart must be preferred.

"I have stored up your word in my heart, that I might not sin against you. Blessed are you, O Lord; teach me your statutes!" (Psalm 119:11).

Where on earth could the Lord locate a people with hearts fixed on the rebirth of righteousness? The time was set for all to obtain salvation, to be forgiven so that the heart of every willing person could go under the knife and be cured of its disease.

"And I will give you a new heart, and a new spirit I will put within you. And I will remove the heart of stone from your flesh" (Ezekiel 36:26).

Everyone who chose God after learning of his love, mercy, and grace would be free. Favor would be distributed in the sight of the Lord. Israel would live, breathe, and teach the Lord's law.

However, Israel was not exempt from the enemy's deceptions and subtle tactics of confusion. Even the elect fell short. Satan's image seemed clearer to some than the image of the God they had chosen to serve. The contusion on mankind's heel pained them severely. If there was anything that could salvage what was left of God's spirit in his creation, the children of earth now required a Savior, a living example of God's law and statutes—an ultimate sacrifice.

> The true light, which gives light to everyone, was coming into the world. He was in the world, and the world was made through him, yet the world did not know him. (John 1:9–10)

> And he shall stand and shepherd his flock in the strength of the Lord; in the majesty of the name of the Lord his God. And they shall dwell secure for now he shall be great to the ends of the earth. (Micah 5:4)

The birth of the king was no secret event. Not all welcomed such precious life into this land. A Savior who would rule over every present and former king struck his enemies breathless. Some were utterly challenged by the prophecy, preceding his existence while others looked forward to it with an earthly eye. No flesh is able to adhere to what is proclaimed from God's spirit.

"Those who are in the flesh cannot please God" (Romans 8:8).

Many law seekers did not appreciate the manifestation of love in the flesh. With an exaggerated opinion of themselves, they had no notion why a Savior was needed to dwell among men in their era.

"The saying is trustworthy and deserving of full acceptance, that Christ Jesus came into the world to save sinners" (1 Timothy 1:15).

The Commander in Chief of God's army entered the war and was prepared for battle. Jesus placed his hands upon the Spirit of God, harmonizing with the fire that sets souls free. As the fulfillment of scriptural prophecy progressed, Satan went into action. It seemed that a man would become weak and worn, enduring extensive abstinence. However, the Spirit of God is willing. When temptation speaks to the flesh, the voice can be pleasant, smooth, and captivating. So the tempter struck, targeting the obvious weakness.

"Each person is tempted when he is lured and enticed by his own desire" (James 1:14).

A man's strength would certainly be fatigued by the sound of subtle deceit. But "not by might, not by power, but by my Spirit, says the Lord of hosts" (Zechariah 4:6). Satan's attempts to subject Jesus to the temptations of a common mortal were shaken off like a daydream, so fleeing became Satan's best option.

"For we do not have a high priest who is unable to sympathize with our weaknesses, but one who in every respect has been tempted as we are, yet without sin" (Hebrews 4:15). The Devil's darts failed hopelessly. Jesus rose higher in the Holy Spirit, allowing God's people to discern how to overcome temptation.

"Did you not know that I must be about my Father's business?" (Luke 2:49).

Earthly ministry was a never-ending work during Christ's lifetime. He approached each situation proclaiming God's love through speech and action.

"Thus also faith, by itself, if it does not have works, is dead" (James 2:17).

Not once did Jesus hold out his hand to heal and return it to his side without glorifying the Father of heaven.

"Truly, truly, I say to you, the Son can do nothing of his own accord, but only what he sees the Father doing. For whatever the Father does, that the Son does likewise" (John 5:19).

The wicked failed to decipher Jesus's approach of bringing the dead to life, of dying to self to be born again. This process would remove the desire for self-righteousness and replace it with a desire for an imputed righteousness that he [Jesus] provides. The Redeemer gained a strange people but lost a chosen group. Some hearts were in the critical stages of iniquity's disease. Their resistance suppressed the love from God's image.

Jesus's ministry continued. Love healed the wounds caused by rejection. Love knew what was in mankind, and that their ways required acts of compassion to guide along the path of acceptance. No one has ever approached love's objective, let alone walked love's journey. Nevertheless, love embraced the challenge in all humility rather than refusing to continue. Love proceeded in belief and hope, with endurance in every step.

Fear the Lord your God. Unfortunately, the teachings of religious leaders concerning reverence to the Almighty struck more distress than warmth of compassion toward a transgressor. God was portrayed as a judge only, not as One who shows mercy. The law was for the people to keep, but it was not for them to bestow righteous judgment. The law was indeed the Word, and the Word became flesh because the written law did not distribute God's mercy. The law merely pointed out the sin; it could not save men from their selfish and unholy natures.

Yes, the wages of sin are to die a certain death, and yes, none are destined to die because every person has opportunities and authority to choose. The Father in heaven would never overwhelm an unwilling individual to partake in salvation, or in his goodness for that matter. However, the mysteries of God's faithfulness, goodness, grace, and mercy were revealed in the Messiah's earthly ministry. The purpose was to help mankind experience the love of God. Law-abiding Jews, unfortunately, misunderstood the Word of God as well as the God they served.

"If I have told you earthly things and you do not believe, how can you believe if I tell you heavenly things?" (John 3:12).

The desires of their flesh were locked in. Satan poisoned the minds of many with his false truth. If God's Word were in men's hearts, his statutes would not be far away; Satan's deception, however, directed men's sights to an empty storehouse, leaving the love of the Father back where he is seated.

"Their end is destruction, their god is their belly, and they glory in their shame, with minds set on earthly things" (Philippians 3:19).

The enemies of Christ were believers of many laws, teachings, and even wonders witnessed with their eyes. The majority believed Jesus was their adversary. Simple dialogues with the Son of Man encouraged witness to the fact that he was real, in the flesh; however, they did not believe this truth.

"If I am not doing the works of my Father, then do not believe in me; but if I do them, even though you do not believe me, believe the works, that you may know and understand that the Father is in me and I am in the Father." (John 10:37-38).

"Whoever believes in me, though he die, yet shall he live, and everyone who lives and believes in me shall never die. Do you believe this?" (John 11:25–26).

Those who would limit the authority and purpose of the Messiah's existence spoke words of disbelief and rejection. Salvation was not sure if their hearts were void of understanding. To believe in Jesus, the heart and mind must be in harmony. No confidence, no trust, no reverence, and no faith yielded no deliverance.

"For God did not send his Son into the world to condemn the world, but in order that the world might be saved through him" (John 3:17).

And so shall that hour be. Time was taken to make God's kingdom practical. Ears tuned in faithfully. Laborers in the vineyard and guests at the wedding feast certainly widened their eyes; two parables Jesus used to explicate his ministry. Surgery was set as the master physician prepared the stage for all to be administered a portion of sanctification.

> If you love me, you will keep my commandments. And I will ask the Father, and he will give you another Helper, to be with you forever. (John 14:15–16)

> And when he comes, he will convict the world concerning sin, and righteousness and judgment. (John 16:8)

> God's love has been poured into our hearts through the Holy Spirit who has been given to us. (Romans 5:5)

> Your lamb shall be without blemish, a male year old. Then they shall take some of the blood and put it on the two doorpost and the lintel of the houses in which they eat it. The blood shall be a sign for you, on the houses where you are. And when I see the blood, I will pass over you, and no plague will befall you to destroy you when I strike the land of Egypt. (Exodus 12:5, 12:7, 12:13)

As the Messiah's earthly ministry drew to a close, signs of weariness and discontent were on display.

> He was despised and rejected—a man of sorrows, acquainted with deepest grief . . . Yet it was our weaknesses he carried; it was our sorrows that weighed him down. (Isaiah 53:2–4 NLT)

> And being in agony he prayed more earnestly; and
> his sweat became like great drops of blood falling down
> to the ground. (Luke 22:44)

Anger, hatred, jealousy, slander, and envy burdened Jesus. Idolatry, impurity, sexual immorality, sensuality, drunkenness, enmity, strife, lies, theft, covetousness—every fleshly desire that causes temptation pressed until his spirit was weighed down, as if gravity itself were magnified ten times upon his steps.

In Old Testament times, animals were hand-picked by the transgressor for atonement through the sacrificial offering. For the final offering, the sacrifice selected himself. According to the logic of sacrificial atonement, Christ was innocent of sin and undeserving of a penalty. Christ was the only one sufficient to be put forward to achieve our salvation. Jesus allowed his capture to embrace his purpose.

"For one will scarcely die for a righteous person—though perhaps for a good person one would dare even to die" (Romans 5:7).

No one would freely choose the fierce task with knowledge of what was to come. However, the reward—reconciliation so that all may obtain justification—meant there was no turning back. Nor would Jesus take matters into his own hands.

> But he was wounded for our transgression; he
> was crushed for our iniquities; upon him was the
> chastisement that brought us peace, and with his stripes
> we are healed. (Isaiah 53:5 NKJV)

> But how then should the scriptures be fulfilled,
> that it must be so. (Matthew 6:54)

> For this is my blood of the covenant, which
> is poured out for many for the forgiveness of sins.
> (Matthew 26:28)

The death of a substitute was not the only step in sacrificial protocol. Sin delivered death. To have life, life was required.

"But you shall not eat flesh with its life, that is, its blood" (Genesis 9:4).

And Jesus would bleed. The Roman guards, fueled with malice and hate, thought it simple to inflict brutal and inhumane treatment upon the Lord. Indirectly, they helped renew sinners when they spilled innocent blood. Demanding Jesus's life, their whips grew thirsty for more, displaying no satisfaction. Lash after lash, bit by bit, until enough was almost too much, Jesus's life flowed from him for the greater good of the very humanity that marveled at his affliction.

So that they may be whole, new, and complete. One can imagine the thoughts of the Messiah as he received their hateful fists, tasteless spit, and even mockery: the crown placed on his head that expelled more of his life for mankind's sake. The blood that once flowed within his body, keeping the Lord stable and at ease, now decorated the city of Jerusalem as a payment for transgression. Unfortunately only few would lay eyes upon it and understand its value. The number of rioters awaiting the death outnumbered those somewhat worthy of being saved. Nonetheless, Jesus would have walked his road for but one follower.

> Greater love has no one than this, that someone lay down his life for his friends. (John 15:13)

> But many were amazed when they saw him! His face was so disfigured he seemed hardly human, and from his appearance, one would scarcely know he was a man. (Isaiah 52:14 NLT)

> Father forgive them, for they know not what they do. (Luke 23:24)

Jesus only knew love. The hurt in his heart was stronger than that which throbbed on his surface. During his darkest hours on the earth, his greatest teaching was this: "But I say to you, love your enemies, bless those who curse you, do good to those who hate you and pray for those who spitefully use you and persecute you . . . For if you love those who love you, what reward have you?" (Matthew 5:44, 5:46 NKJV).

The time came that there was barely any more life to spill, he had taken responsibility for all sins, and nothing remained but to complete what he had started. Ironically, completion would set forth another beginning.

"It is finished" cried the Savior, and the sacrifice was accepted. Death surrounded his presence.

"For our sake he made him to be sin who knew no sin, so that in him we might become the righteousness of God" (2 Corinthians 5:21).

The perfect image, a just man, a teacher, lover of all, leader throughout eternity, a man who knew everyone's sin but his own, was laid to rest for the righteousness that men would never achieve on their own.

"We have all become like one who is unclean and all our righteous deeds are like a polluted garment" (Isaiah 64:6).

Some spent the next day in sorrow. It was the Lord's Day; thus universal rest was acknowledged, and none would step outside, even the Son of Man who once proclaimed, "For the Son of Man is lord of the Sabbath" (Matthew 12:8). But early "on the first day of the week . . . while it was still dark" (John 20:1), some traveled in eagerness to visit Jesus's tomb—only to find it empty.

> Why do you seek the living among the dead? (Luke 24:5)
> For this perishable body must put on the imperishable, and this mortal body must put on immortality. (1 Corinthians 15:53)

Jesus did the unthinkable. Though he had spoken the truth that he would be raised on the third day, no one had perceived his resurrection as imminent. His demise was witnessed.

O death, where is your victory? O death, where is your sting? (1 Corinthians 15:55)

More than that, we also rejoice in God through our Lord Jesus Christ, through whom we have now received reconciliation. (Romans 5:11)

The road to recovery ends when those on earth who belong to God in heaven are reunited in paradise. The setback is removing the heart disease for which sin offerings could not excuse. Redemption was made when the cross lifted the sacrifice between heaven and earth. God's people recognized what it took to be cleansed; they can all look and be healed.

And I, when I am lifted up from the earth, will draw all people to myself. (John 12:32)

Now the salvation and the power and the kingdom of our God and the authority of his Christ have come, for the accuser of our brothers has been thrown down, who accuses them day and night before our God. And they have conquered him by the blood of the Lamb and by the word of their testimony, for they loved not their lives even unto death. (Revelation 12:9–11)

For the grace of God appeared bringing salvation for all people. (Titus 2:11)

And all flesh shall see the salvation of God. (Luke 3:6)

EPILOGUE

When men began populating the earth, each one ran after his heart's desire. We see a great example of this during the episode at the Tower of Babel (Genesis 11). They obeyed whatever desire nurtured their beliefs. For instance, Abel gave a firstborn lamb because he believed in his Creator's words (Genesis 4). Peter went for his sword to defend himself because in his heart he was a defender and he valued his life (John 18). Saul of Tarsus persecuted Christ's followers because he believed in the order of the Pharisees (Acts 9).

We see that in our creation lies a piece of us that has to obey. We are obligated to satisfy our hearts; we are required to validate the dearest affirmatives we crave. Our hearts form our beliefs. Then we know we can strive toward, reach, and conquer anything we seek because we believe in it. Those who believe in success will obey the lessons that create success. If someone has a void he believes must be filled with love, he will seek and stalk whatever resembles his view of what love is.

This is exactly why there are criminals whose loved ones cry out, "I never knew he was capable of doing that." It is because whatever we believe, we are geared toward committing the actions necessary to that belief. If our beliefs are obedient to the wrong desire, it does not necessarily mean that we are abominations. This could signify that the correct choices have yet to be revealed as

71

correct. Once revealed, explained, and accepted, the new believer can apply the belief and walk in the new way of submission, like Saul of Tarsus.

The word *submissive* is beyond comparison. When there is agreement, there is no resistance or struggle, only agreement. God wants us to be aware that whatever we believe in, we will obey that belief, because desire has an almost irremovable place in the heart. "Truly, truly, I say to you, everyone who commits a sin is a slave to sin" (John 8:34), because we have no choice but to obey what we have a desire for. My English teacher was the greatest at her job because she believed that she could teach anyone how to be great in English.

My mission is not to change someone's mind. I don't expect my belief will instantly influence others so that we are one-sided, working toward the same change in everyone else. My task is to present the words of wisdom, display righteousness's character, and leave the mind-changing to the only One qualified for that job. The Holy Spirit is the mystery of won hearts, changed motives, honest intentions, and enlightened paths. So long as my task is not complete, the Spirit's task is challenged to enlighten the mistaken other.

The best way to convince someone else to choose to obey is for me to choose to obey. I have to trust God's statutes for my life, and my heart has to be entrapped in his holiness. If I fail to believe in one area of the Lord's teachings, I'll accept an alternate road leading in my own direction, forgetting submissiveness. That is how sin started. Accept only nine out of ten of God's laws and statutes, and self-centered behavior is born. *I won't steal, that's not in me. Nor are murder and slander. But why can't I just tell one small lie and color up what is already true? Why not do this thing once?* It's because law is law with no shades of gray. There is no compromising what is true and what is false.

God is holy. What makes him holy is his flawless inability to do anything other than good. He is good because there is nothing else to associate him with. If something is not like him, it is obviously not good. Also, if all that is being asked is permission to do something (anything) once, then it must be suspiciously immoral to choose to perform it regularly.

I need not explain how repetition causes objectives to become easier. That's exactly how we become great, and we know that. What no one strives for is becoming great at mistakes. Christ gave us a direction so that we may become great at walking toward greatness.

Glory!

About the Author

LaDell Farrar discovered a passion for writing after his first year at Maryville University. A psychology major as well as a layman in the Christian church, he has devoted time to studying basic examples that associate scientific and creationist points of view. LaDell currently resides in St. Louis, Missouri, where he commits to ministry in several areas of his local church. Working in the church initiated a substantial amount of learning that he found appropriate for explaining everyday struggles and conquering those challenges. This was found to be applicable to the average person because of the universality we share ascending from the first being. Therefore, LaDell compiled his knowledge into *Building the Body of Christ*.

CPSIA information can be obtained at www.ICGtesting.com
Printed in the USA
LVOW08s1006260714

396061LV00001B/22/P